HEXAGON
happenings
15 quilts & projects

by Carolyn Forster

Landauer Publishing, LLC

Hexagon *happenings*
By Carolyn Forster

Copyright © 2014 by Landauer Publishing, LLC
Hexagon Happenings projects
Copyright © 2013 by Carolyn Forster

This book was designed, produced,
and published by Landauer Publishing, LLC
3100 101st Street, Urbandale, IA 50322
www.landauerpub.com
515/287/2144   800/557/2144

President/Publisher: Jeramy Lanigan Landauer
Vice President of Sales and Administration: Kitty Jacobson
Editor: Jeri Simon
Art Director: Laurel Albright
Photographer: Sue Voegtlin

ISBN 13: 978-1-935726-66-1

Library of Congress Control Number: 2014946873
This book printed on acid-free paper.
Printed in United States

10-9-8-7-6-5-4-3-2-1

About the Author

Carolyn Forster, quilt maker, teacher and author, has been sewing and creating for as long as she can remember. Since stitching her first quilt from 1" fabric squares at the age of 17, she has been hooked on patchwork and quilting.

Carolyn's love of quilting sends her to many places teaching, lecturing and sharing her favorite quilting techniques. She has authored a number of patchwork and quilting books in the UK and America. Carolyn lives in Royal Tunbridge Wells, in the south east of England, with her husband and son, and a lot of fabric.

To find out more about hexagons, or to contact Carolyn about classes, go to:
www.carolynforster.co.uk
E-mail: carolynforster@hotmail.co.uk
or write to her at:
23 Woodbury Park Road
Tunbridge Wells, Kent
TN4 9NQ, UK

  FACEBOOK.COM/
LANDAUERPUBLISHING

 YOUTUBE.COM/
LANDAUERPUBLISHING

PINTEREST.COM/
LANDAUERPUB   2

Contents

Introduction

I love the look of hexagon quilts, especially those from the 1930's and earlier. Their soft colors and rich patterns have always drawn me.

In fact, one of my first stitching projects was the classic hexagon pincushion made with two grandmother's flower garden rosettes. My first quilt was even created using the English Paper Piecing method we often associate with hexagon and mosaic patchwork. I enjoyed cutting the fabric and paper, wrapping each one like a little parcel before whip stitching them together.

Like so many stitchers I soon found there were other methods to sew fabric patches together, and I began exploring those as well. I still dabbled in hexagons, but nothing really inspired me to finish an entire quilt.

In the 1980's I discovered pre-cut fabric hexagons. Surely this was the boost I needed to complete a quilt. I experimented with hand sewing the hexagons without the papers and on the sewing machine, but to this day that quilt top is still not quilted.

While I did discover that hexagons did not have to be stitched around paper, the process still didn't move quite fast enough for me. I soon realized that if I just made my hexagons bigger and stitched them on the machine, things would move more quickly and all the ideas and projects I wanted to try could be accomplished.

Although I love to piece by hand and machine, I really love the quilting aspect. And, by making things bigger, I could get to the quilting sooner. In addition, if everything could be rotary cut with no math, then it would be even quicker. That is when I realized I could make my hexagon quilts happen, and you can too.

Hexagon, diamond, equilateral triangle and kite shapes are used in the projects. By simplifying my approach and working with one set of shapes I could concentrate on the designs, fabric choices and quick stitching.

Rotary cutting the shapes is easy when you use the templates provided. The templates also include the seam allowance so you can machine or hand stitch the shapes together. These interconnecting shapes provide endless design opportunities.

There is a vast array of hexagon quilts to turn to for inspiration. I encourage you to look at antique quilts and draw inspiration to design your own hexagon quilts. Here and on the following pages I have included photographs of antique quilts that inspired some of the projects in the book.

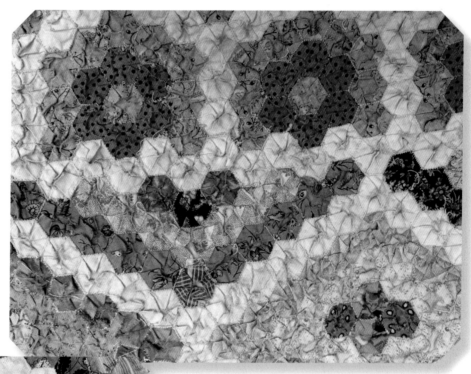

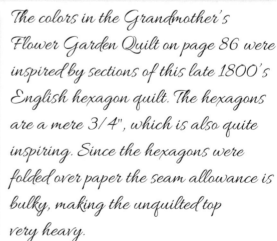

The colors in the Grandmother's Flower Garden Quilt on page 86 were inspired by sections of this late 1800's English hexagon quilt. The hexagons are a mere 3/4", which is also quite inspiring. Since the hexagons were folded over paper the seam allowance is bulky, making the unquilted top very heavy.

This very simple strip quilt was
the starting point for my Strippy
Hexagons and Diamonds Quilt
on page 106.

This scrappy kite quilt from
the late 1930's inspired
the Blueberry Jam Quilt
on page 120.

This English quilt from the early 1900's was the starting point for the Hexagon Honeycomb Quilt on page 82.

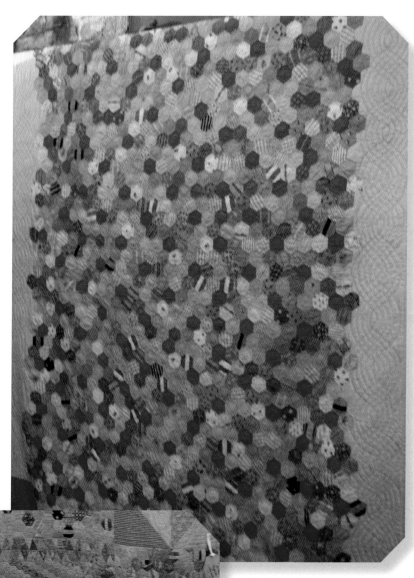

The colors in the Boxed Hexagon Quilt on page 138 were inspired by this amazing English medallion quilt.

Hexagon Basics

Hexagon quilts are simple to create when the hexagons are big and pieced together on the sewing machine. Using templates can also be a huge time saver.

Acrylic templates are ideal for the projects in this book, but certainly not necessary. This section will show you how to cut hexagons with and without templates, how to make your own templates and how to draft hexagons in any size desired.

It is also a good idea to check with your favorite quilt shop, since there are tools available that incorporate multiple hexagon sizes within one ruler. Experiment with different methods to make your hexagons and then choose the one that works best for you. Personally, I prefer the templates. I can simply cut and sew without worrying about following the correct lines.

Piecing the hexagons together on the sewing machine is also a great way to speed up the process. When time is not a factor the pieces can be hand stitched. Hand stitching the hexagon projects is very easy and it makes the process portable and sociable. I use the American piecing method and do not insert papers into the shapes, which makes the project come together more quickly. As many of you already know, the seam allowances are not sewn through when hand piecing, making it easy to set in pieces.

General Hints and Tips for Sewing a Hexagon Project

- The fabric quantities given for each project are the amount of fabric used in the actual design. When you are buying fabric you may want to add 10-20 percent to allow for any shrinkage in pre-washing, any bits of fabric lost when you are rotary cutting to straighten the fabric, and any cutting or sewing mistakes.

- When you stop sewing at the 1/4" mark, remove the work from the machine leaving approximately 1" to 2" of trailing thread. The extra thread will keep the stitches from coming undone if they get pulled. I prefer to do this rather than making securing or backstitches on the machine. This often adds bulk to the seam and allows for no flexibility when setting in the hexagons.

- To achieve greater accuracy when stopping and pivoting to set in seams, use a shorter stitch length on your machine.

- The instructions tell you to mark the 1/4" starting and stopping points on the shapes. After some practice and with the help of your 1/4" piecing foot, you will be able to gauge the 1/4" seam without marking.

- When placing hexagons on a quilt top's straight edge, try to place the hexagon's straight of grain side along this edge. This will help stabilize the straight side of the quilt top.

- You will be working with a number of bias edges due to the shapes. Try using spray starch on the shapes to help stabilize the fabrics.

Drafting Hexagon Shapes

There are dozens of hexagon templates and tools available for our convenience, but it is still important to understand how to make basic hexagon shapes. This knowledge will allow you to create shapes in any size, which will give you greater freedom when designing your own quilts.

After drafting the hexagon, it can be divided into the basic shapes needed to make the quilts in this book—diamonds, equilateral triangles and kites. All you need to do is add 1/4" seam allowances.

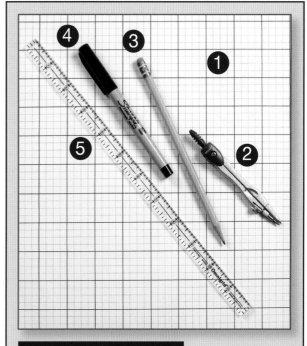

Materials

1. 1/4" gridded graph paper

2. Compass

3. Pencil

4. Fine Permanent Marker

5. Acrylic Quilter's Ruler

Drafting Hexagon Shapes

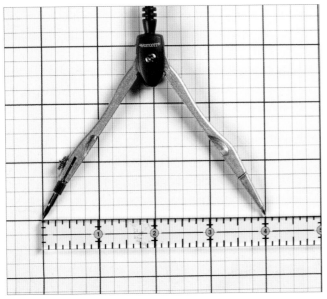

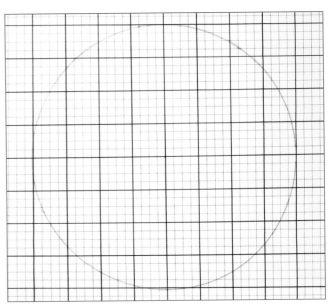

1 Adjust the compass points to the length of one side of your desired hexagon. Our example uses 4". This measurement will create the hexagon shapes in the quilt projects.

2 Place the point of the compass in the center of the grid paper and draw a circle.

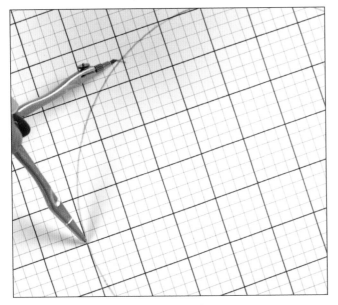

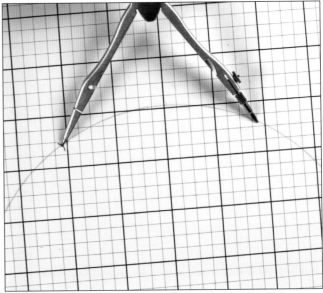

3 Leaving the compass set at the same distance (4"), place the point on the circumference of the circle where the center lines intersect.

Turn the compass to draw through the circle on each side of the compass point.

4 Move the compass point to the opposite end of the same line and draw through the circle again.

Drafting Hexagon Shapes continued

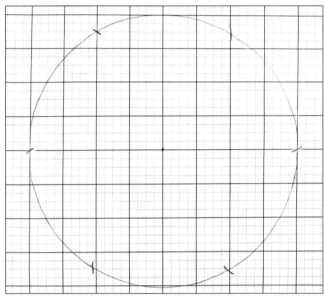

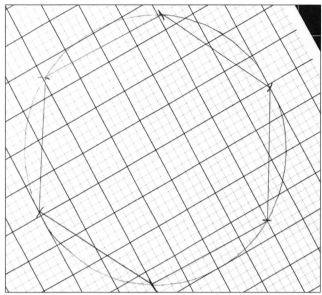

5 Mark each of these points clearly with a pen, as well as the points where the compass was placed. There should be six marks an equal distance apart. Mark the center of the circle also.

6 Using a pencil and ruler, join the points together to create a basic hexagon shape.

The hexagon is drawn to finished size. A 1/4" seam allowance needs to be added for rotary cutting and stitching.

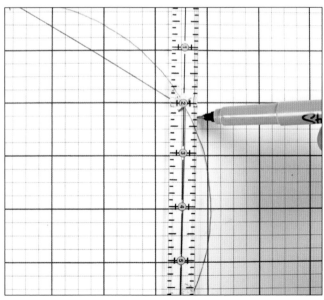

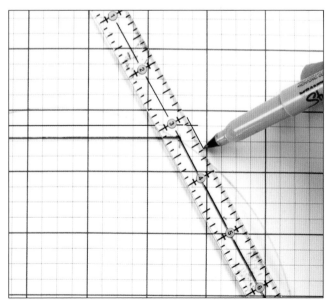

 7 Place the 1/4" line of a quilter's ruler on the drawn line and mark the length of the side with a fine permanent marker. Continue marking 1/4" around the entire hexagon. The hexagon can be cut out and used as a template for your projects or you can divide it to create other basic shapes.

Note: Always angle the permanent marker toward the ruler's edge. If you angle it away from the ruler, the seam allowance will actually be larger than 1/4".

Drafting Diamonds and Equilateral Triangles

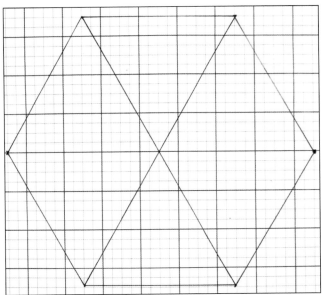 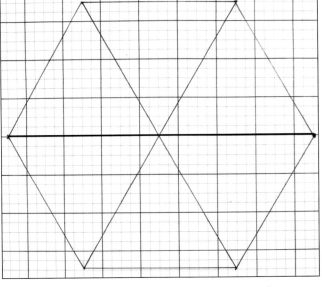

1 The simplest way to draft diamond and triangle shapes is to divide the hexagon shape. To make diamond shapes connect opposite corners of the hexagon by drawing lines through the middle as shown.

2 To create equilateral triangles, draw a line through the center of the diamonds.

Drafting Kite Shapes

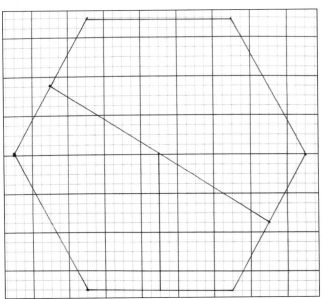 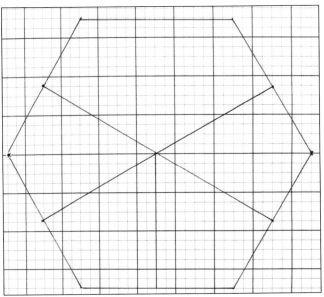

1 To make the kite shapes from a hexagon, find the halfway point along each straight side and mark. In our example it is 2". Drafting the hexagon on gridded paper allows you to check the measurements easily. Draw lines to connect the halfway points as shown.

Rotary Cutting Shapes with Acrylic Templates

The projects in this book are designed using four common shapes—hexagon, equilateral triangle, diamond and kite. These shapes can all be cut with a rotary cutter, ensuring a high level of accuracy. No math or worrying about lining up the correct lines; you simply need to cut around the shapes.

There are many hexagon rulers available and if you are already comfortable working with one of them, there is no reason not to continue. However, I needed to simplify my approach and found that working with one set of ready cut shapes allowed me to concentrate on my designs, fabric choices and quick stitching techniques.

No doubt, you will discover many opportunities to use these interconnecting shapes in your own designs.

Tips on Rotary Cutting

- Always remember to cut away from your body. Never cut toward or across your body.

- It may be useful to use a spinning rotary cutting mat.

- The instructions given are for right-handed cutting. Reverse the instructions if you are left-handed.

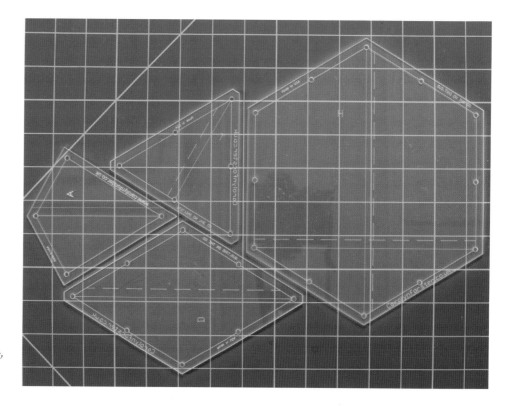

The projects in this book are designed using four common shapes—hexagon, equilateral triangle, diamond and kite.

Cutting Hexagon Shapes *(Note: wof = width of fabric)*

1 Cut a 7-1/2" x wof strip. Lay the strip horizontally on a cutting mat with the selvage to your left. Place the hexagon template on the strip near the selvage as shown. Do not place the template over the selvage.

2 Using a rotary cutter, cut along the right side of the hexagon template as shown.

3 Turn the fabric and template 180-degrees.

4 Cut along the right side of the template to create a hexagon shape.

5 Place the hexagon template on the fabric strip and continue cutting hexagon shapes in the same manner.

Cutting Triangle Shapes *(Note: wof = width of fabric)*

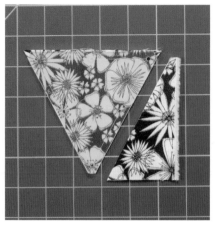

1 Cut a 4" x wof strip. Lay the strip horizontally on a cutting mat with the selvage to your left. Place the triangle template on the strip near the selvage as shown. Do not place the template over the selvage.

2 Using a rotary cutter, cut along the right side of the triangle template as shown.

3 Turn the fabric and template 180-degrees. Cut along the right side of the template to create a triangle shape.

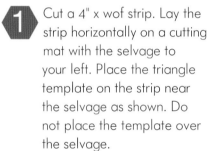

4 Place the triangle template on the fabric strip, matching straight edges, and continue to cut triangle shapes in the same manner.

5 Trim the tails as you cut the triangles or go back and cut them all at once. This will assist you when matching the shapes for piecing.

Cutting Partial Hexagon Shapes (Note: wof = width of fabric)

Partial hexagons are great for filling in the outside edges of hexagon projects when a straight side is required.

1 Cut a 2-5/8" x wof strip. Lay the strip horizontally on a cutting mat with the selvage to your left. Place the hexagon template's dashed line on the straight edge of the strip as shown. This ensures that seam allowance is added to the shape; the solid line is the actual size of the partial hexagon. Do not place the template over the selvage.

2 Using a rotary cutter, cut along the right side of the hexagon template as shown.

3 Turn the fabric and template 180-degrees. Cut along the right side of the template to create a partial hexagon shape.

4 Place the hexagon template on the fabric strip, matching straight edges and realigning the dashed line on the template with the raw edge of the fabric strip. Continue to cut partial hexagon shapes in the same manner.

5 If you didn't trim the tails as you were cutting the partial hexagons, go back and cut them now. This will assist you when matching the shapes for piecing.

Cutting Kite Shapes *(Note: wof = width of fabric)*

1 Cut a 3-5/8" x wof strip. Lay the strip horizontally on a cutting mat with the selvage to your left. Place the kite template on the strip near the selvage as shown. Do not place the template over the selvage.

2 Using a rotary cutter, cut along the right side of the kite template as shown.

3 Turn the fabric and template 180-degrees.

4 Cut along the right side of the template to create a kite shape.

5 Place the kite template on the fabric strip matching straight edges, and cut along the right edge of the template. Continue cutting kite shapes in the same manner.

Cutting Half Hexagon Shapes *(Note: wof = width of fabric)*

It often makes more sense to cut a partial shape instead of cutting a full one and trimming it later. It also saves fabric and time. Half hexagons are another great way to create a straight edge on a hexagon project.

1 Cut a 4" x wof strip. Lay the strip horizontally on a cutting mat with the selvage to your left. Place the hexagon template's dashed line on the straight edge of the strip as shown. This ensures that seam allowance is added to the shape; the solid line is the actual size of the half hexagon. Do not place the template over the selvage.

2 Using a rotary cutter, cut along the right side of the hexagon template as shown.

3 Turn the fabric and template 180-degrees. Cut along the right side of the template to create a half hexagon shape.

4 Place the hexagon template on the fabric strip, matching straight edges and realigning the dashed line on the template with the raw edge of the fabric strip. Continue to cut half hexagon shapes in the same manner.

5 Trim the tails as you cut the half hexagons or go back and cut them all at once. This will assist you when matching the shapes for piecing.

18

Cutting Diamond Shapes *(Note: wof = width of fabric)*

1 Cut a 4" x wof strip. Lay the strip horizontally on a cutting mat with the selvage to your left. Place the diamond template on the strip near the selvage as shown. Do not place the template over the selvage.

2 Using a rotary cutter, cut along the right side of the diamond template as shown.

3 Turn the fabric and template 180-degrees.

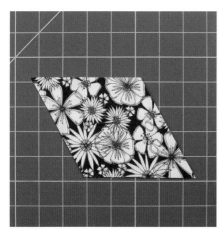

4 Cut along the right side of the template to create a diamond shape.

5 Place the diamond template on the fabric strip, matching straight edges, and continue to cut diamond shapes in the same manner.

6 Trim the tails as you cut the diamonds or go back and cut them all at once. This will assist you when matching the shapes for piecing.

Cutting Half Diamond Shapes *(Note: wof = width of fabric)*

Half diamond shapes can be added to the ends of rows of hexagons to achieve a straight edge. These shapes can be made with the diamond or hexagon template. Our example uses the diamond template.

1 Cut a 2-5/8" x wof strip. Lay the strip horizontally on a cutting mat with the selvage to your left. Place the diamond template's dashed line on the straight edge of the strip as shown. This ensures that seam allowance is added to the shape; the solid line is the actual size of the half diamond. Do not place the template over the selvage.

2 Using a rotary cutter, cut along the right side of the diamond template as shown.

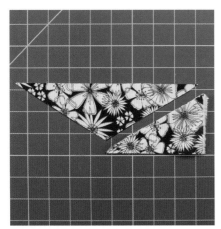

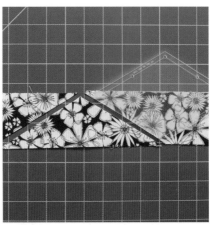

3 Turn the fabric and template 180-degrees. Cut along the right side of the template to create a half diamond shape.

4 Place the diamond template on the fabric strip, matching straight edges and realigning the dashed line on the template with the raw edge of the fabric strip. Continue to cut half diamond shapes in the same manner.

5 Trim the tails as you cut the half diamonds or go back and cut them all at once. This will assist you when matching the shapes for piecing.

Number of Shapes from Fabric Strips

Each project in the book lists fabric requirements and the number of shapes to cut. Once you are comfortable sewing with hexagons, you may want to design your own projects.

The information listed below tells you how many shapes can be cut from fabric strips. All information is based on 40"-wide usable fabric.

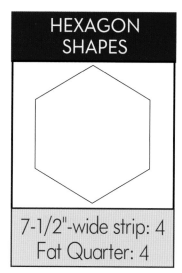

HEXAGON SHAPES

7-1/2"-wide strip: 4
Fat Quarter: 4

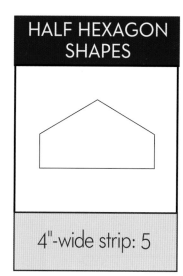

HALF HEXAGON SHAPES

4"-wide strip: 5

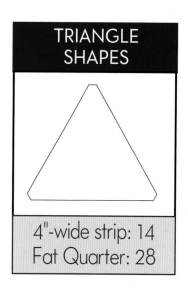

TRIANGLE SHAPES

4"-wide strip: 14
Fat Quarter: 28

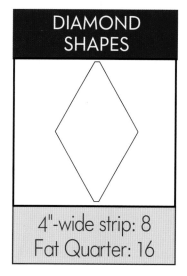

DIAMOND SHAPES

4"-wide strip: 8
Fat Quarter: 16

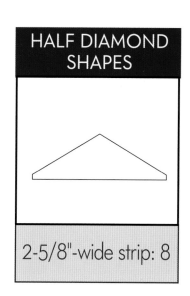

HALF DIAMOND SHAPES

2-5/8"-wide strip: 8

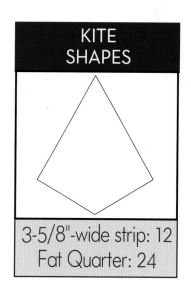

KITE SHAPES

3-5/8"-wide strip: 12
Fat Quarter: 24

Making the Templates

If you are not using the acrylic templates, you can create your own templates using the shapes in the book. Two of the most common methods used to create templates are given.

Tracing shapes onto template plastic

1 Lay template plastic over the shapes in the book.

2 Trace the shapes directly onto template plastic using a fine-tip permanent marker. Be sure to transfer ALL the template markings.

3 Use a small sharp scissors to cut out the shapes.

4 Use a small hole punch to mark the 1/4" seam allowance points.

Photocopying shapes

1 Photocopy the templates from the book onto copy paper. Check the copy against the book to make sure it is accurate.

2 Rough cut around the template leaving an extra 1/2" or so around the outside of the template.

3 Glue the right side of the paper template onto template plastic to assist with accuracy when cutting.

4 Use a small sharp scissors to cut out the shapes directly on the lines.

5 Use a small hole punch to mark the 1/4" seam allowance points.

6 Turn the template over and transfer any remaining markings before removing the paper.

Tips for Accuracy

- To stabilize the template on the fabric, place a few pieces of double-sided tape to the back of the template. You can also spritz it with 404® Spray and Fix Repositional Craft Adhesive.

- Place the fabric on a sheet of fine sandpaper to prevent it from moving as you draw around the template. The sandpaper will grip the fabric and keep it in place. You can also use a rotary mat, a Matilda's own Design Mat or a sheet of ROC-LON® multipurpose cloth™ to place the fabric on while drawing around the template.

- Cut the fabric directly on the drawn line. If you cut outside the line, the shapes will be larger; if you cut inside the line, the shapes will be smaller.

- When drawing around the template, always angle the pencil in toward the template to be the most accurate. If you angle the pencil away from the template, the shape will be larger than what is needed.

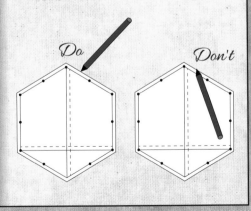

Do   Don't

Using the Templates

Templates made with template plastic are not meant to be used with a rotary cutter. It is too easy to slip with a rotary cutter and cause injury.

1 Place the template on the fabric and draw around the shape with a fine sharp pencil that will show up on the fabric.

Note: It does not matter if you draw on the right or wrong side of the fabric since the drawn line is the cutting line.

2 Cut out the fabric shape directly on the drawn line with a sharp fabric scissors.

3 Mark the 1/4" seam allowances through the holes in the template.

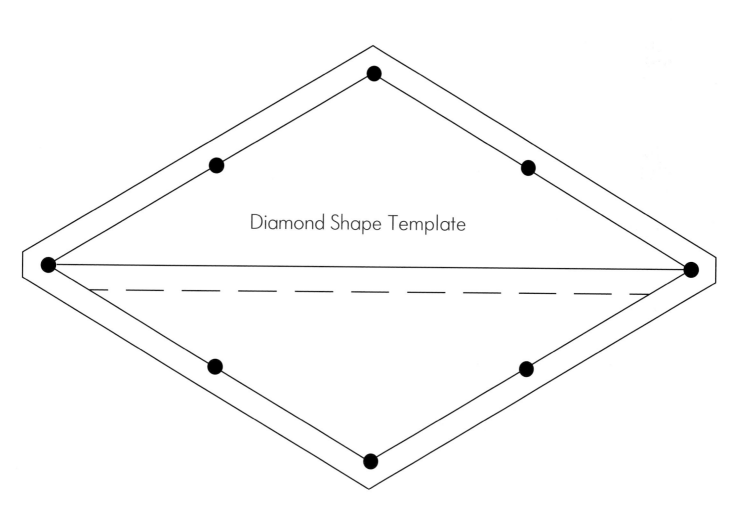

Diamond Shape Template

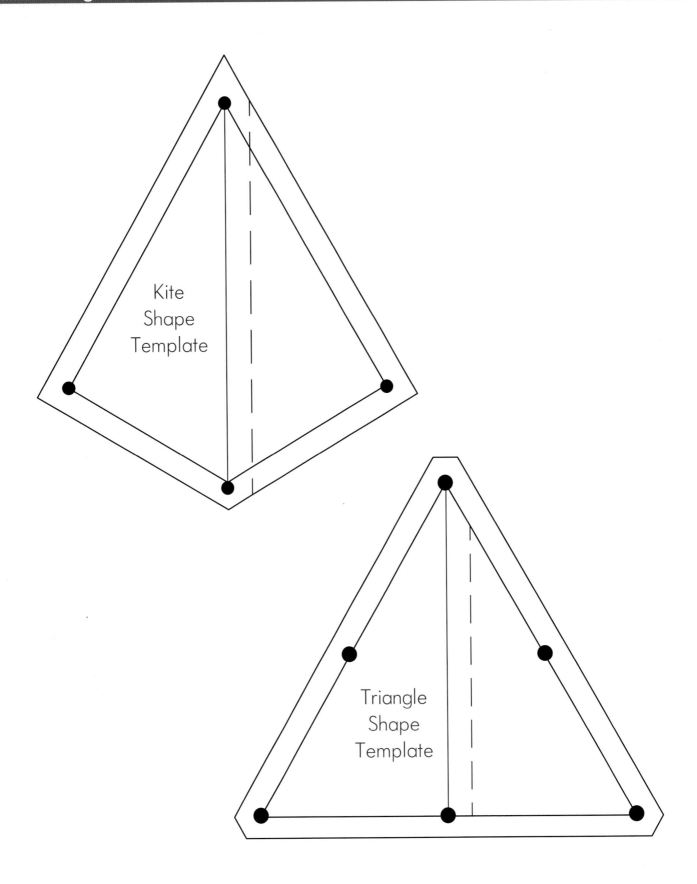

Kite
Shape
Template

Triangle
Shape
Template

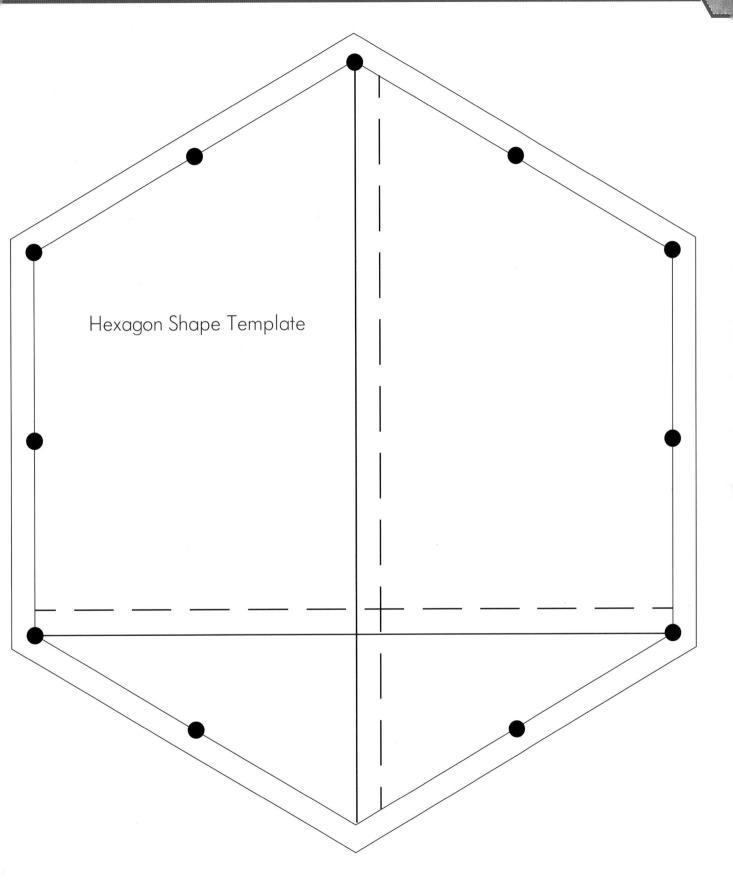

Hexagon Shape Template

Cutting Shapes without Templates

The hexagon, diamond and triangle are basic shapes that can create an endless variety of designs. While using the acrylic templates is the simplest way to cut the shapes, it is important to know how to cut the shapes using only a ruler and rotary cutter. It will allow you to cut shapes any size needed for your project design.

Cutting Equilateral Triangles

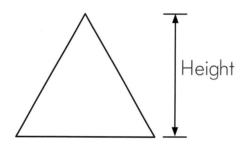

Height

Cutting Diamonds (60°)

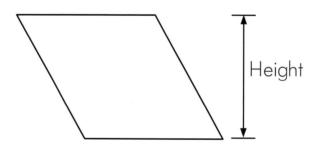

Height

Cutting Hexagons

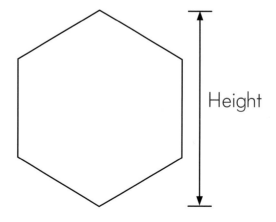

Height

Cutting Hexagons without Templates

Determine the finished height of the hexagon needed and add 1/2". This measurement allows for seam allowance and is the width the fabric strips are cut. For example, in the steps shown the desired finished hexagon is 7" tall so the fabric strips are cut 7-1/2"-wide.

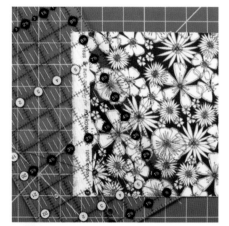

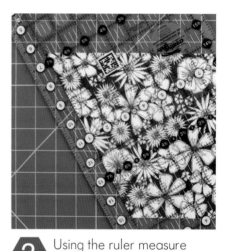

1 Cut a fabric strip 7-1/2"-wide. Place the strip along a horizontal line on the cutting mat. Angle the acrylic ruler so the 60-degree line is along the same horizontal line as the fabric strip.

2 Cut along the right edge of the ruler to remove the selvage.

3 Using the ruler measure 7-1/2" from the cut edge as shown.

Note: If the ruler is not wide enough, you may need to butt two rulers together.

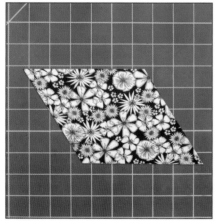

4 Cut along the right side of the ruler to create a diamond.

5 Align the points of the diamond shape along a vertical line on the cutting mat.

Cutting Hexagons without Templates continued

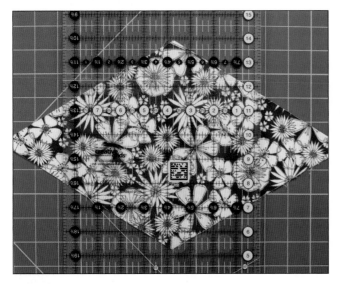

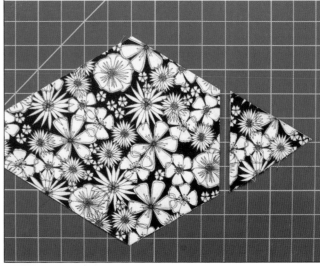

6 Measure the width of the diamond shape and divide in half. In the example, the measurement is 3-3/4". Align the 3-3/4" line on the ruler along the same vertical line on the mat as the diamond points.

7 Cut along the right edge of the ruler.

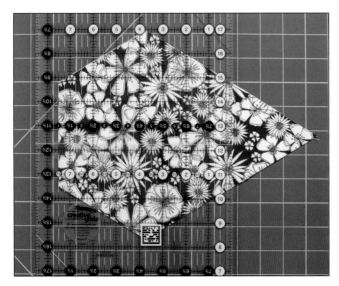

8 Rotate the shape 180-degrees and repeat steps 5-6 to make the hexagon shape.

Note: If you prefer, you can align the 7-1/2" mark on the ruler on the left side of the shape and cut along the ruler's right edge.

Cutting Equilateral Triangles without Templates

Determine the finished height of the triangle needed and add 3/4". This measurement allows for seam allowance and is the width the fabric strips are cut. For example, in the steps shown, the desired finished triangle is 3-1/2" tall so the fabric strips are cut 4-1/4"-wide.

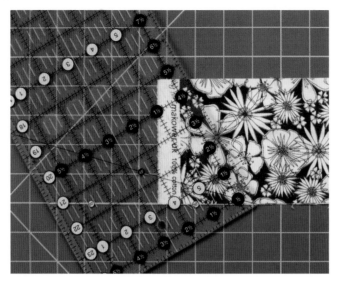 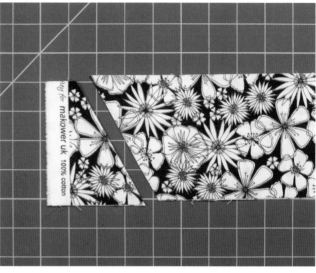

1 Cut a fabric strip 4-1/4"-wide. Place the strip along a horizontal line on the cutting mat. Angle the acrylic ruler so the 60-degree line is along the same horizontal line as the fabric strip. Cut along the right edge of the ruler to remove the selvage.

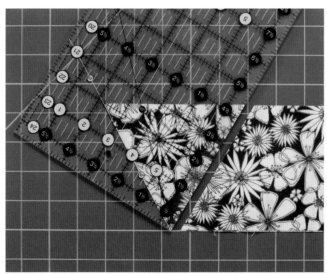 

2 Turn the ruler and align the 60-degree line with the previous cut as shown. Cut along the right edge of the ruler to make an equilateral triangle.

3 Continue cutting triangles in the same manner. Always check to be certain the ruler's 60-degree line is accurately aligned.

Cutting 60-degree Diamonds without Templates

Determine the finished height of the diamond needed and add 1/2". This measurement allows for seam allowance and is the width the fabric strips are cut. For example, in the steps shown the desired finished height of the diamond is 3-1/2" so the fabric strips are cut 4"-wide.

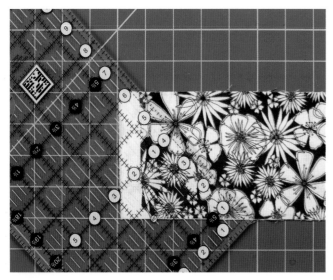 

1 Cut a fabric strip 4"-wide. Place the strip along a horizontal line on the cutting mat. Angle the acrylic ruler so the 60-degree line is along the same horizontal line as the fabric strip. Cut along the right edge of the ruler to remove the selvage. The 60-degree lines on the cutting mat can be used to check accuracy if needed.

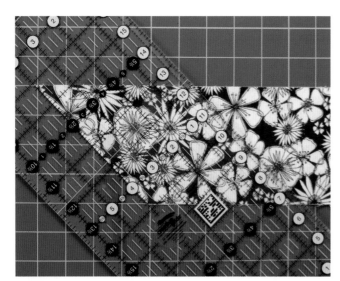 

2 Keeping the ruler's 60-degree line on the bottom edge of the fabric, measure 4" from the cut edge as shown. Cut along the right side of the ruler to make a 60-degree diamond.

3 Continue cutting diamonds in the same manner. Always check to be certain the ruler's 60-degree line and 4" mark are accurately aligned.

Cutting 60-degree Diamonds from Jelly Roll Strips

If you are not using jelly roll strips, cut 2-1/2"-wide fabric strips. A 2-1/2"-wide ruler is very helpful when cutting diamonds from the strips since it can act as a template when cutting.

Note: If you do not have a 2-1/2"-wide ruler, see the tip on page 32 for using a larger ruler.

1 Place the strip along a horizontal line on the cutting mat. Angle the acrylic ruler so the 60-degree line is along the same horizontal line as the fabric strip.

2 Cut along the right edge of the ruler to remove the selvage. The 60-degree lines on the cutting mat can be used to check accuracy if needed.

3 Keeping the ruler's 60-degree line on the bottom edge of the fabric, measure 2-1/2" from the cut edge as shown. Cut along the right side of the ruler to make a 60-degree diamond.

4 Continue cutting diamonds in the same manner. Always check to be certain the ruler's 60-degree line and 2-1/2" mark are accurately aligned.

Cutting 60-degree Diamonds from 2-1/4" Strips

A narrow ruler is helpful when cutting diamonds from 2-1/4"-wide strips. If you do not have a narrow ruler, see the tip on using a larger ruler.

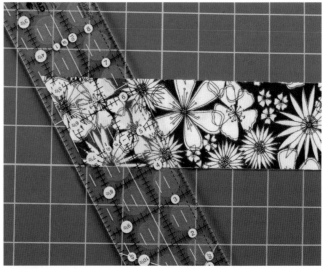

1 Cut 2-1/4"-wide strips of fabric. Place a fabric strip along a horizontal line on the cutting mat. Angle the acrylic ruler so the 60-degree line is along the same horizontal line as the fabric strip. Cut along the right edge of the ruler to remove the selvage. The 60-degree lines on the cutting mat can be used to check accuracy if needed.

2 Keeping the ruler's 60-degree line on the bottom edge of the fabric, measure 2-1/4" from the cut edge as shown. Cut along the right side of the ruler to make a 60-degree diamond.

Tip
- If using a large ruler, mark the 2-1/4" and 60-degree lines with masking tape. This will assist you in correctly aligning the ruler on the fabric strip.

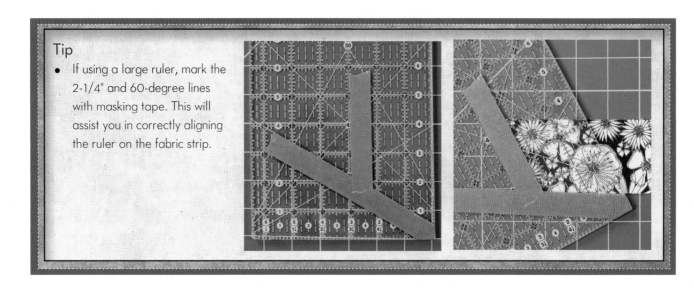

Selecting Fabrics

The projects in this book are created using large hexagons. This allows you to experiment with various fabric and scale combinations for maximum visual impact and immediate effect. The size of the hexagons and other shapes also gives you the opportunity to work through your stash and, of course, add new fabrics along the way.

A few of the projects require a large quantity of fabric. Do not let this deter you. Simply mix similar fabrics together to achieve the yardage needed.

The Grandmother's Flower Garden Quilt on page 86 is a good example. I did not have enough fabric to make the six petals in each flower the same, so I chose similar prints and alternated them around each central hexagon. The different fabrics in the flower petals added interest to the quilt.

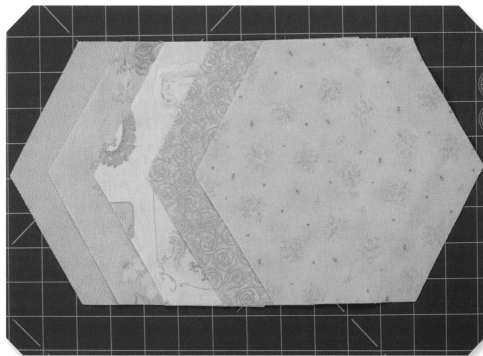

While I had enough of the same fabric for the background, I have made other Grandmother's Flower Garden quilts using several prints in the same tone for the background.

Selecting Fabrics continued

Use different scales of print in a single quilt to keep the eye moving. The Hexagon Honeycomb quilt on page 82 uses a multitude of prints in a variety of blue fabrics. Even though the quilt is made only of hexagons, the variety in the scales of print provides interest.

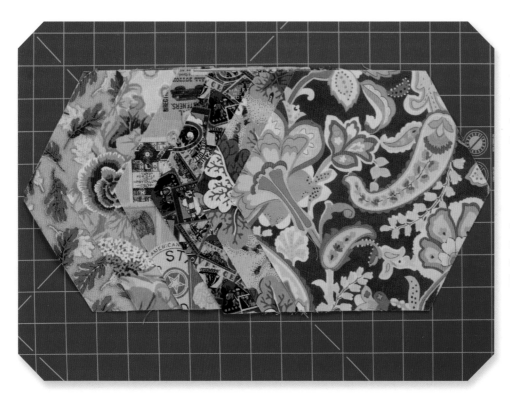

The mere size of the hexagons encourages you to show off your favorite large-scale prints.

Play around with different fabrics, print scales and colors to create a quilt that is both interesting and unique.

Selecting Fabrics continued

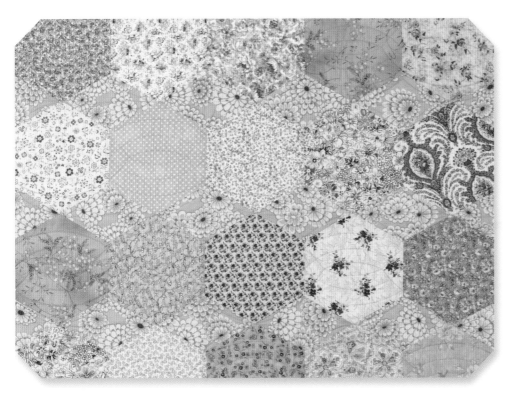

The tonal colors in the Strippy Hexagons and Diamonds Quilt on page 106 keeps the design blurred and restful.

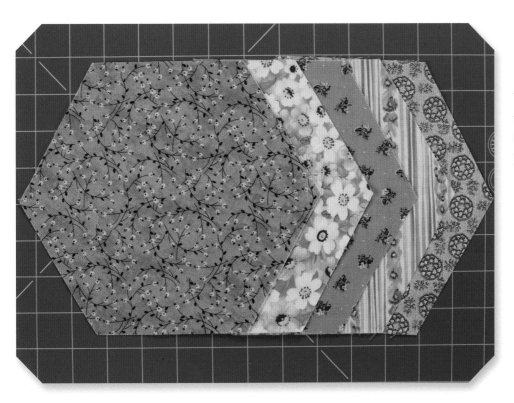

This selection of lilac fabrics illustrates a similar idea regarding print scale.

Selecting Fabrics continued

A more dramatic design is created when using higher contrast fabrics for the diamonds.

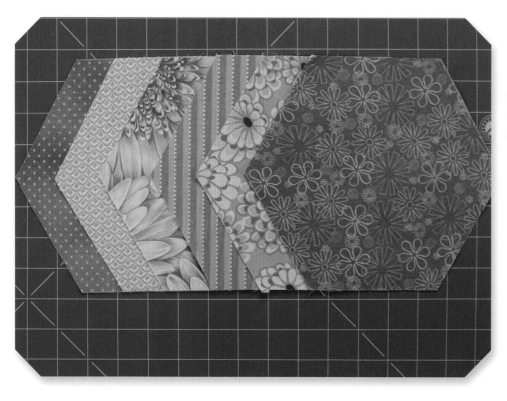

Use a variety of prints, including stripes, dots and florals, within one quilt for interest.

Selecting Fabrics continued

The Stars and Cubes quilt
on page 130 shows
how white provides a great
contrast to scraps.

To create a fresh
modern look, use white
with a variety of solids.

Machine Sewing Hexagons

Stitching the hexagons together on the sewing machine allows you to finish projects quickly. The steps given use only four hexagons and show how to set them in. After some practice you will be able to sew rows of hexagons together easily.

Note: The sewing technique shown is also used when sewing rows of hexagons together. You will alternate between seeing the open seam and having it hidden.

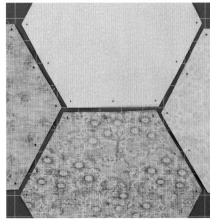
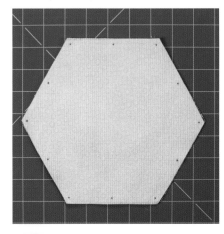

1 Cut out four hexagons using the templates on page 25. Refer to Making the Templates on page 22. Using the holes in the template, mark the 1/4" seam allowances on the wrong side of the hexagons.

2 Lay out the hexagons as shown.

3 Layer the center hexagons, right sides together. Stitch the hexagons together along one edge, starting and stopping at the 1/4" seam mark. Do not sew through the seam allowance.

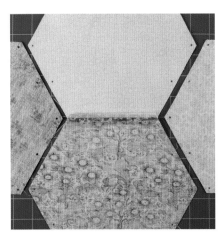

4 Press the seam open.

5 With right sides together, place one of the remaining hexagons on the sewn hexagons in step 3, matching raw edges.

Machine Sewing Hexagons continued

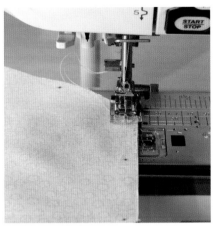

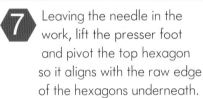

6 With the sewn hexagons on the bottom, begin sewing at the 1/4" mark. Stop stitching when you reach the opposite 1/4" mark. The mark will be above the open seam of the sewn hexagons. This will allow you to pivot everything in order to turn the corner.

7 Leaving the needle in the work, lift the presser foot and pivot the top hexagon so it aligns with the raw edge of the hexagons underneath.

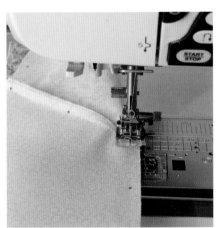

8 Push the bottom stitched hexagons toward the back of the presser foot to alleviate bulk or pleating at the needle. Lower the presser foot and continue sewing to the 1/4" mark. Press the seams open.

9 Layer the sewn piece and remaining hexagon right sides together, matching raw edges. In this case, you will be stitching with the single hexagon on the bottom.

Machine Sewing Hexagons continued

10 Begin sewing at the 1/4" mark. Stop stitching when you reach the opposite 1/4" mark. The mark will be above the open seam of the sewn hexagons. This will allow you to pivot everything in order to turn the corner.

11 Leaving the needle in the work, lift the presser foot and pivot the hexagons as before.

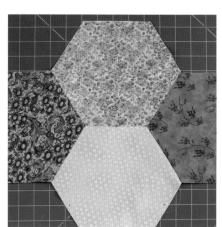

12 Continue sewing to the 1/4" mark.

13 Press the seams open.

Quick Tablemat

After sewing the four hexagons together, turn them into a fun tablemat. Make several to practice setting in hexagons. The tablemats will eat into your stash and make great gifts.

Finishing Material

25" x 20" backing fabric

25" x 20" batting

1/2 yard binding

From binding fabric, cut:
2-1/2" bias strips to equal approximately 60".

1. Layer the hexagon top, batting and backing together. Baste the layers together using your favorite basting technique. Since this was a small project I used 505® Spray and Fix.

2. Quilt as desired. The tablemat shown was quilted using a straight stitch on the machine. Each stitched line is approximately a presser foot apart. Refer to pages 64-69 for more quilting ideas.

3. Trim the backing and batting even with the tablemat top.

4. Sew the bias binding strips together on the diagonal to make one long continuous strip. Press the strip in half, wrong sides together, along the length.

5. Sew the bias binding to the mat referring to page 59.

Hand Sewing Hexagons

Although sewing the hexagon projects by machine is quick and convenient, it is only convenient if you are sitting in front of your sewing machine. Fortunately, sewing shapes together by hand is simple and easy. Best of all, you can combine the machine and hand sewn shapes in your project without any problems, giving you ultimate flexibility.

Hand Piecing Tips

- Use a neutral color sewing thread so the stitches blend in with the fabrics. A contrasting thread was used in the steps to illustrate the stitching process.

- Before stitching, mark the beginning and ending 1/4" seam allowance points on the wrong side of the shape. It is also helpful to mark a dashed line between the seam allowance points. This will provide a straight line on which to sew. After some hand stitching practice, you will not need the extra marks and will be able to gauge the 1/4" seam allowance by eye.

- Since all the shapes are a uniform size, you will only need to mark the 1/4" seam allowance points and stitching line on the top shape. After aligning the shapes' raw edges, you will automatically be sewing in the correct place on the bottom one.

- Start and stop sewing at the 1/4" seam allowance marks. Do not sew through the seam allowance. This will make setting in the pieces and sewing around corners much easier. Often, it will also make it unnecessary to press seams open.

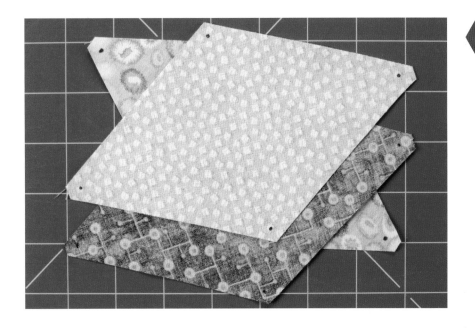

1 Cut out three diamonds using the templates on page 23. Refer to Making the Templates on page 22. Using the holes in the template, mark the 1/4" seam allowances on the wrong side of the diamonds.

Hand Sewing Hexagons continued

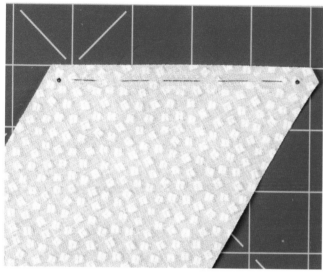

2 Draw a dashed line between the seam allowance marks on one of the diamonds. This will be the sewing line.

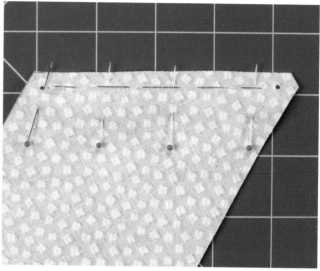

3 Layer the marked diamond on another diamond, right sides together. Match up the raw edges and pin the shapes together into the seam allowance.

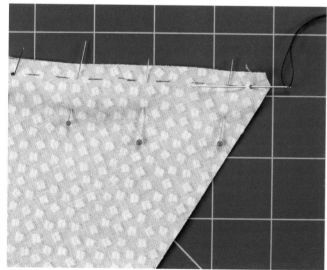

4 Cut a length of sewing thread approximately 18" and knot the end. Begin sewing at the 1/4" seam allowance mark using a backstitch for extra security.

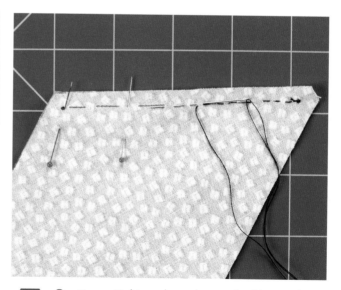

5 Continue stitching along the marked line with a small running stitch, removing pins as you come to them. While stitching, backstitch every inch or so to stop the thread from gathering when you pull the stitches.

Hand Sewing Hexagons continued

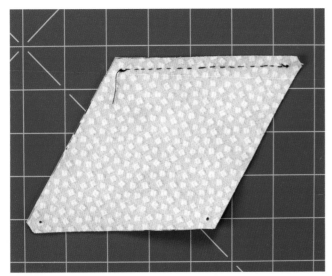

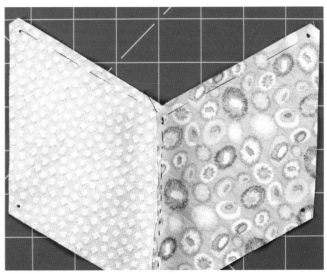

6 Continue sewing to the opposite 1/4" seam allowance mark. Make three small backstitches before cutting the thread, leaving a 1" tail.

7 Open the sewn pieces and lay right side down on a flat surface. Mark the stitching lines on the wrong side of the pieces.

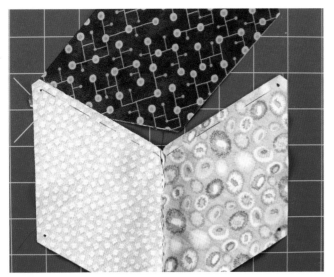

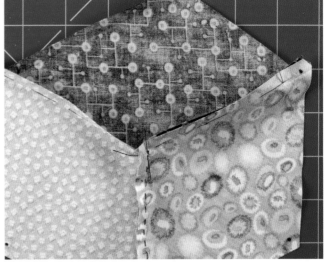

8 Lay the third diamond under the sewn pieces, right sides together and matching raw edges. Pin the pieces together along one edge and into the seam allowance.

Hand Sewing Hexagons continued

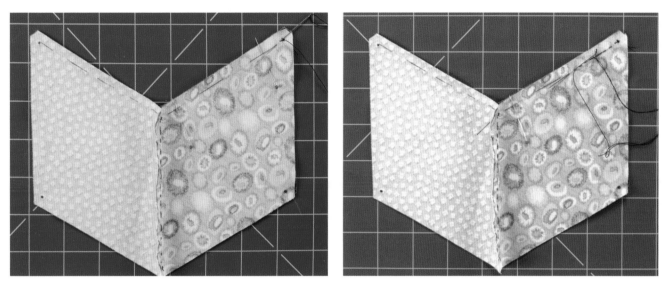

9 Begin stitching at the outside edge, adding a backstitch for extra security. Continue stitching toward the inside corner, taking a backstitch every inch or so.

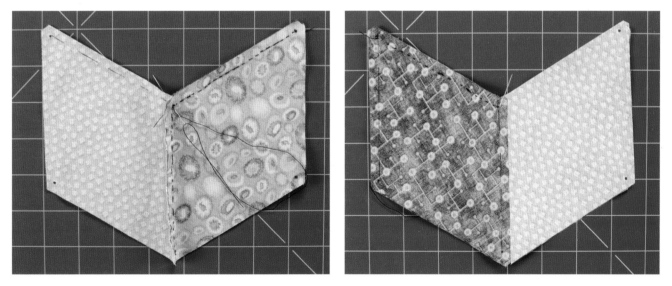

10 When you come to the corner make a backstitch and pull the needle through to the back.

Hand Sewing Hexagons continued

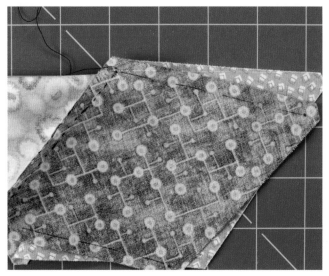

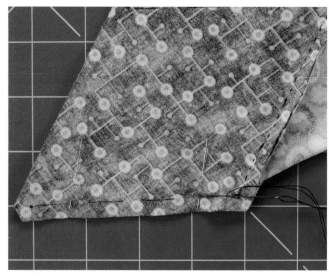

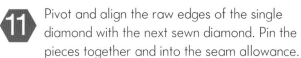 Pivot and align the raw edges of the single diamond with the next sewn diamond. Pin the pieces together and into the seam allowance.

12 Make a backstitch at the 1/4" starting mark and pull tight. This will eliminate any gaps at the inside corner.

13 Continue stitching to the opposite 1/4" mark. Make three small backstitches before cutting the thread.

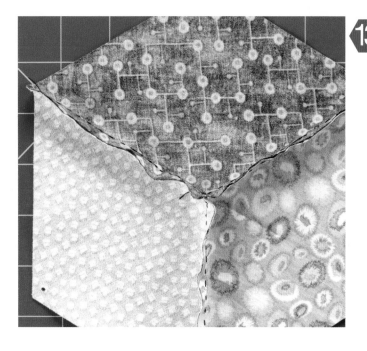

Hand Sewing Hexagons continued

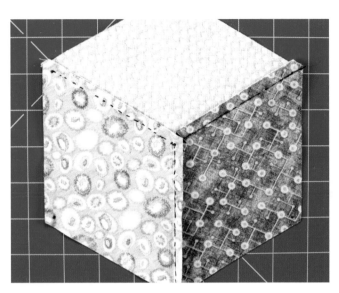
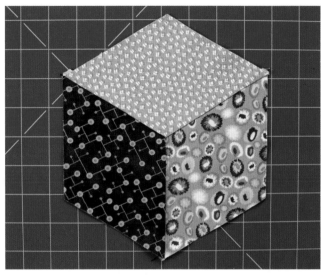

 To complete the hexagon, press the pieces following the individual project instructions. While you do not need to press the seams open, you will want to press seams in a consistent direction.

This basic hand sewing method will work for all the projects in this book. Remember, you can combine hand and machine sewn pieces in your projects.

Finishing and Binding Hexagon Quilt Edges

Finishing the edges on a hexagon quilt can be as simple as trimming off the hexagon peaks. Personally, I like the interesting shape the hexagons create along the quilt edge.

While there are many ways to finish a hexagon quilt, the ones I most commonly use are outlined for you on the following pages.

Each of the projects in the book specify how it was finished but any of the techniques shown will work, so feel free to experiment.

Bias binding makes quick work of the hexagons' peaks and inside corners. If you prefer to skip the binding process, try the turned through edge finish technique on page 56.

Straightening Hexagon Quilt Edges by Trimming

One of the quickest ways to finish a hexagon quilt edge is to trim the hexagons to create straight sides. You can then add borders or bind the quilt. The trimming can be done before or after layering and quilting the project.

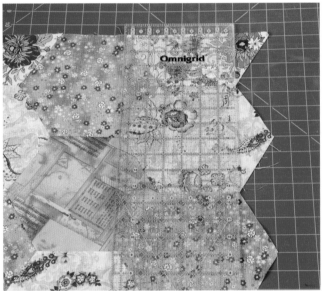

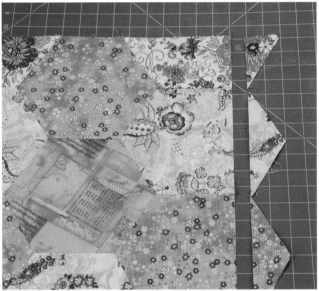

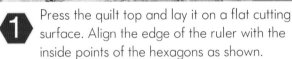

1 Press the quilt top and lay it on a flat cutting surface. Align the edge of the ruler with the inside points of the hexagons as shown.

2 Using a rotary cutter, trim along the right edge of the ruler to remove the hexagon "peaks". Continue to trim each side of the quilt top in the same manner.

Note: If the quilt top is too large for the cutting surface it will need to be trimmed in sections. Realign the quilt top and ruler on the cutting surface after each section is trimmed.

3 After the quilt top edges have been trimmed, borders can be added if desired. If you are not adding borders, the quilt top is ready to be layered, quilted and bound.

Note: To stabilize the outside edges of the quilt top, use a long machine stitch and sew 1/8" from the raw edge all the way around the quilt top.

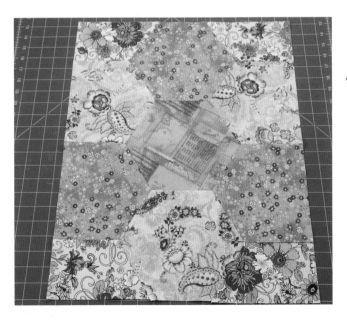

Straightening Hexagon Quilt Edges with Inserts

Inserting half and partial hexagons along the edges of a hexagon quilt will create a straight edge. This is helpful if you don't want to bind a quilt with numerous corners and miters. The Zigzag Diamonds Quilt on page 100 is an example of a quilt top with inserts.

The steps in the example use one fabric for the inserts. If a wide variety of fabrics are used in the quilt you may wish to cut the inserts from a selection of fabrics to continue the look. After setting in the inserts to straighten the sides of the quilt top you can add borders or layer, quilt and bind it.

Note: When sewing the inserts to one side of the quilt top, the bulk of the quilt top will be on the bed of the sewing machine. When sewing inserts to the other side of the quilt top the insert will be on the bed of the machine.

1 Determine the number of half and partial hexagons needed to straighten the quilt edges. The example shown uses four half hexagons and six partial hexagons. Cut out the half and partial hexagons using the template on page 25. Refer to Making the Templates on page 22. Using the holes in the template, mark the 1/4" seam allowances on the wrong side of the shapes. Lay out the quilt top and half and partial hexagon shapes as shown.

2 Layer a half hexagon on the quilt top, right sides together and matching raw edges as shown. Stitch the pieces beginning at the right edge 1/4" mark. Stop stitching at the opposite 1/4" seam mark. The mark will be above the open seam of the sewn hexagons on the quilt top. This will allow you to pivot everything in order to turn the corner. Do not sew through the seam allowance.

3 Leaving the needle in the work, lift the presser foot and pivot the half hexagon so it aligns with the raw edge of the hexagon underneath.

Straightening Hexagon Quilt Edges with Inserts continued

4 Push the quilt top underneath toward the back of the presser foot to alleviate bulk or pleating at the needle. Lower the presser foot and continue sewing to the end of the pieces.

5 Press the first sewn seam open and the second seam to one side.

Note: The first seam is pressed open because a partial hexagon will be added to that side.

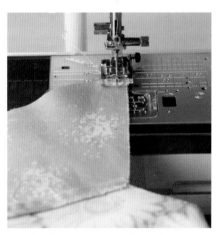

6 Stitch the remaining half hexagons in place referring to steps 2-5.

7 Layer a partial hexagon on the quilt top, right sides together and matching raw edges as shown.

8 Begin sewing through the seam allowance at the top edge of the quilt top.

Note: When sewing the pieces together the quilt top is on top and the partial hexagon is on the bottom.

Straightening Hexagon Quilt Edges with Inserts continued

 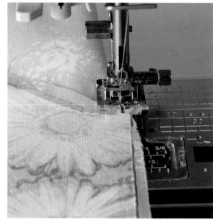 

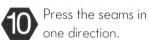

9 Continue sewing to the center of the open seam. Leaving the needle in the work, lift the presser foot and pivot the pieces as before, aligning the raw edges. Continue sewing to the end of the pieces.

10 Press the seams in one direction.

11 Working around the quilt, sew the remaining partial hexagons in place. Press after adding each one.

After the inserts have been sewn in and the quilt top is straight, borders can be added if desired. If you are not adding borders, the quilt top is ready to be layered, quilted and bound.

Straightening Hexagon Quilt Edges with Appliqué

It is possible to straighten the sides of a hexagon quilt by appliquéing the edges to a straight border. After the straight edges are created, more borders can be added or the quilt top can be layered, quilted and bound.

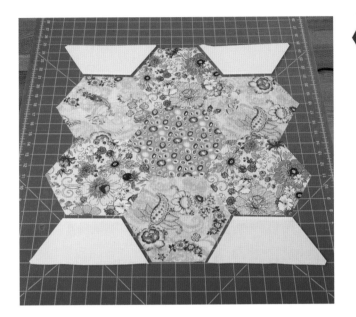

1 Lay the quilt top on a flat surface and determine where half hexagons can be inserted to straighten an edge. Cut the number of half hexagons needed using the template on page 25. Refer to Making the Templates on page 22. Using the holes in the template, mark the 1/4" seam allowances on the wrong side of the shapes.

Note: Inserting half hexagons wherever possible lessens the amount of fabric waste.

2 Referring to Straightening Hexagon Quilt Edges with Inserts on page 50, sew the half hexagons in place.

3 Lay the quilt top on the border fabric, right sides up, to help determine the width of border that will look best with the quilt top. Adjust the border fabric until it is the desired width. The border can be any width you choose as long as you have enough fabric.

Straightening Hexagon Quilt Edges with Appliqué continued

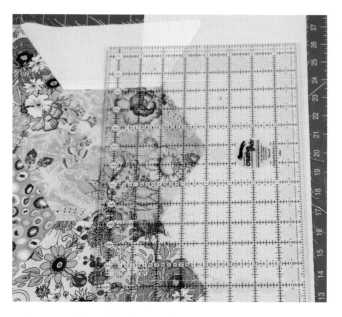

4 Using a ruler, measure from the peak of the hexagons to the desired size of the border. A 4"-wide finished border is used in the example. To determine the width to cut the border strips, follow the formula given.

  4" finished border width

+ 2" measurement from hexagon
  peak to inside corner

+ 1/4" outside edge seam allowance

+ 1" hexagon/border overlap
_____

7-1/4"- wide border strips

Measure the length of the quilt top and add 1" to the measurement. Cut the border strips to this length.

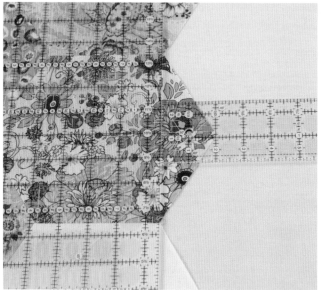

Straightening Hexagon Quilt Edges with Appliqué continued

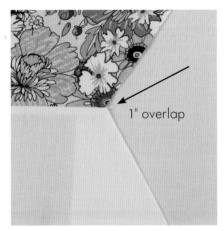

1" overlap

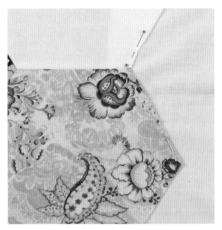

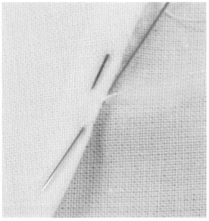

5 Place one border strip on a flat surface, right side up. Lay the quilt top, right side up, on the border strip overlapping the edge by 1". There should be an equal amount of border fabric extending over each edge. This will be trimmed after the sides are appliquéd.

6 Turn under the quilt edge 1/4" and pin in place. Since the seams have been pressed open the quilt edge should fold neatly at the inside corners.

7 Using a small slipstitch, appliqué the quilt top and border strip together. Be sure to use a thread that will blend with the fabrics.

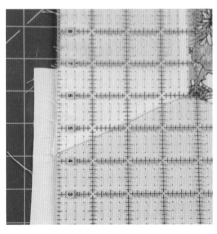

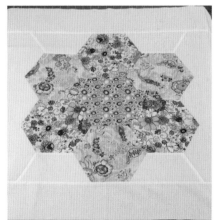

8 Trim the border edges even with the quilt top.

9 In the same manner add the remaining border strip to the opposite side of the quilt top.

10 Trim any excess fabric from the back of the quilt top, lining up the 1/4" seam allowances. Press.

11 To add borders to the remaining sides of the quilt top, use the original finished border width and add 1/2". In the example, the border strips are 4-1/2"-wide by length of quilt top. Sew the border strips to opposite sides of the quilt top. Press seams away from the quilt top.

Turned Through Edge Finish for Hexagon Quilts

The turned through edge finish technique gives quilts a sharp finish and lets you bind the quilt before it is quilted. It works well with quilts that are going to be tied or big stitch quilted.

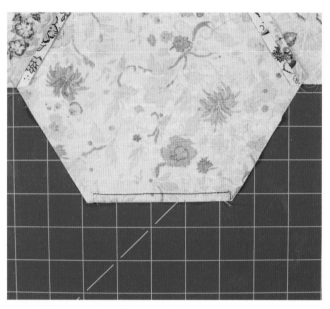

1 Using a 1/4" seam, stitch a line along one of the hexagon's straight sides. The line should be approximately 4" long. The stitch line will strengthen the fabric for turning through and create a neat, clean finish.

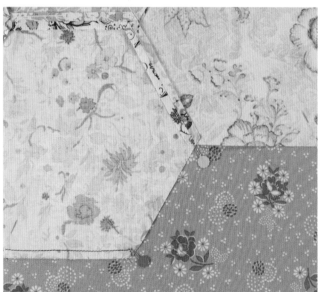

2 Smooth the batting out on a flat surface. Place the backing fabric right side up on top of the batting. Smooth out any wrinkles. Center the quilt top, right side down, on the backing. Pin the layers together at each hexagon peak and inside corner. If the quilt has straight sides, pin every 6".

3 With a walking foot, begin stitching at one end of the reinforced stitched line using a 1/4" seam allowance. Backstitch the beginning few stitches. Remove the pins as you come to them.

Turned Through Edge Finish for Hexagon Quilts continued

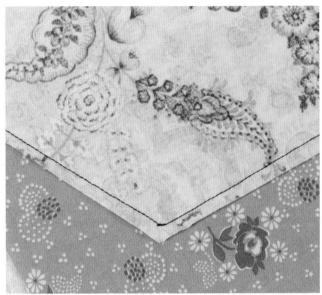

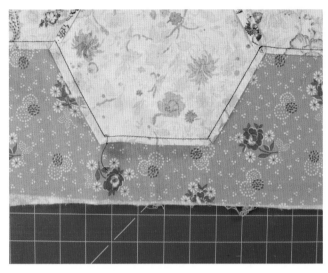

4 As you reach each turn, stop stitching and leave the needle in the layers. Lift the presser foot, pivot the layers and lower the presser foot to continue stitching. At each corner, stitch two or three stitches across it for a neater corner when turning the quilt through.

5 Stop stitching when you reach the beginning of the reinforced stitch line. Backstitch the ending stitches to secure them.

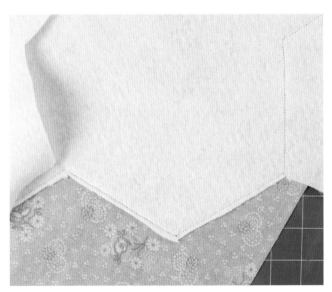

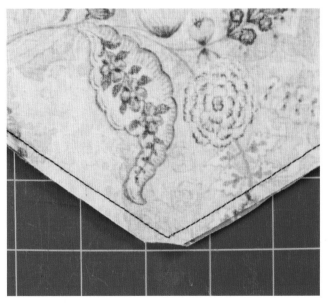

6 Trim the batting close to the stitching line.

7 Trim the quilt back leaving a 1/4" seam allowance. Snip diagonally across the corners through the layers to minimize any bulk.

Turned Through Edge Finish for Hexagon Quilts continued

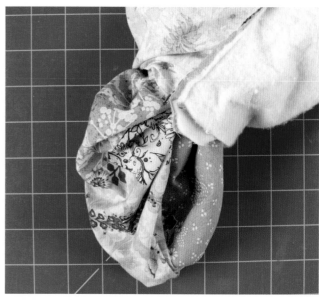

8 Carefully snip at the inside corners to create a smoother finish when the quilt is turned through.

9 Turn the quilt right side out through the reinforced stitch opening. Carefully ease the quilt through the opening.

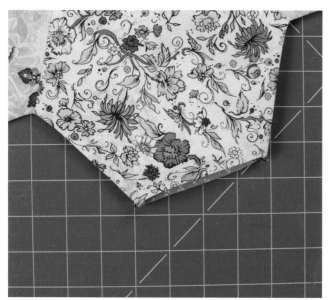

11 Secure the layers by stitching 1/4" around the outside edge of the quilt.

Pin baste the layers together before quilting or tying the quilt.

10 Poke the corners out and roll the seam between your thumb and forefinger to help it lay flat. Use pins or hemming clips to keep the edges flat. Fold the raw edges of the opening under. Using a slipstitch, stitch the opening closed.

Bias Binding for Hexagon Quilts

Binding a hexagon quilt is much easier when using fabric strips cut on the bias grain. Bias binding has more stretch allowing it to go smoothly around the peaks and inside corners of the hexagons. The binding can be sewn to the quilt by hand or machine.

Note: I use the walking foot on my sewing machine to sew the binding to the quilt. I align the edge of the quilt and binding with the side of the foot as I stitch. Experiment on your machine to see which guide gives you the finished binding width you desire.

Tips on Calculating Binding

- To calculate how much binding is needed, I measure each side of the quilt and add the measurements together. This tells me how many inches of binding I need to go around the quilt. I add an extra 10" just to be safe.

- When the sides of your quilt are not straight, as is often the case with a hexagon quilt, measure the uneven sides as you would the straight sides. Multiply the measurement by 1.5 to calculate the number of inches needed for binding on each uneven side.

- Another guide to consider is from every yard (1m) of fabric you can cut approximately 10 yards (10m) of binding. That should be enough for any quilt.

1 To determine the true bias of the fabric, fold the fabric edge over to meet the selvage. The diagonal fold is the true bias. Using a rotary cutter and ruler, cut off the fold.

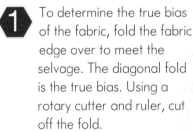
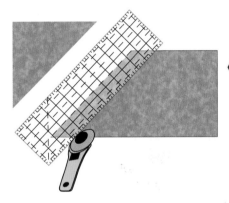

2 Cut the number of bias binding strips needed for your project. I generally cut my binding strips 2-1/2"-wide.

3 To join the bias binding strips into one continuous strip, overlap the ends of two strips at a 90-degree angle, right sides together.

Bias Binding for Hexagon Quilts continued

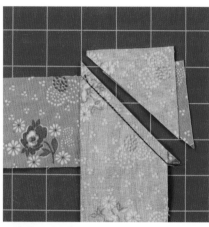

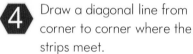

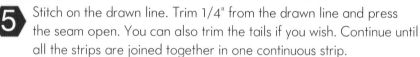

4 Draw a diagonal line from corner to corner where the strips meet.

5 Stitch on the drawn line. Trim 1/4" from the drawn line and press the seam open. You can also trim the tails if you wish. Continue until all the strips are joined together in one continuous strip.

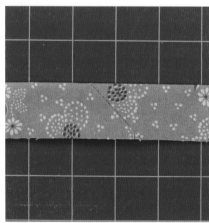

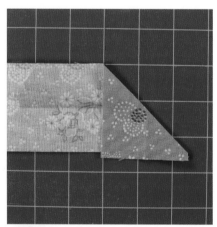

6 Fold the binding strip in half along the long edge, wrong sides together. Press along the entire length.

7 Unfold the binding strip and fold one end at a 45-degree angle. Press.

8 Trim 1/4" from the pressed fold.

Bias Binding for Hexagon Quilts continued

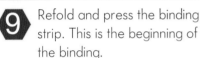

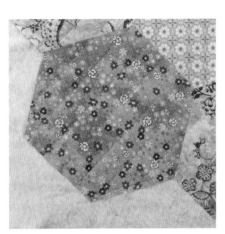

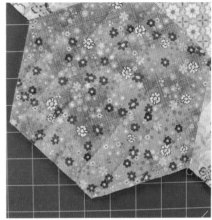

9 Refold and press the binding strip. This is the beginning of the binding.

10 Layer the quilt top, batting and backing. Quilt the layers. To prepare the quilt for binding, trim the batting and backing even with the quilt top.

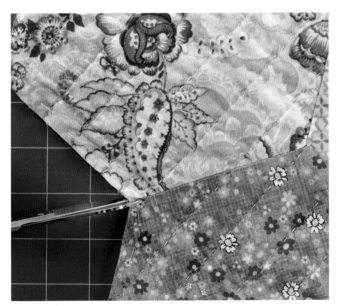

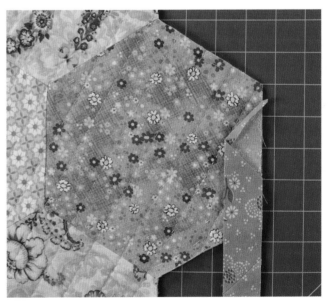

11 Carefully snip the inside corners of the batting and backing fabric. The quilt top should not need to be snipped since the sewing stopped at the 1/4" mark. If you forgot to stop sewing at the 1/4" mark, it is okay to snip the top as well.

12 The binding will be attached to the front of the quilt first. Align the raw edge of the binding strip with the raw edge of the quilt top. If there is a long straight side on the quilt, begin the binding strip at its center. If the sides are uneven, such as a hexagon quilt, start the binding strip in the center of a hexagon side as shown.

Bias Binding for Hexagon Quilts continued

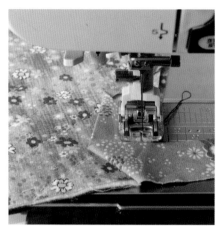

13 Begin stitching approximately 1/2" from the angled edge. Stop stitching 1/4" from the peak (outside corner) so it can be mitered. To mark the 1/4" as you near the corner, fold the binding up so its raw edge is aligned with the raw edge of the quilt top. Finger-press the fold creating a crease. Put the binding back down and stitch to the crease line. Add a few securing stitches at the crease.

14 Remove the quilt from under the presser foot. Fold the binding up so all raw edges align.

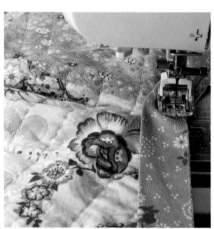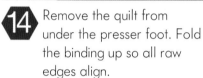

15 Fold the binding strip back onto the quilt top matching up the raw edges along the next edge. Begin stitching from the edge of the quilt and binding to secure the fold. Repeat this at each peak as you sew the binding to the quilt.

16 The inside corners also need to be mitered. As you approach the inside corners, stop stitching and fold the binding back to align with the inside corner's seam line. Finger-press the crease. Replace the binding and stitch to the crease line.

17 Leaving the needle down in the crease, lift the presser foot and straighten the quilt edge. Do this by gathering the bulk of the quilt to the left of the foot. The quilt edge will straighten because you have snipped into the quilt. Keep the bulk behind the needle so you do not sew a pleat into the quilt.

Bias Binding for Hexagon Quilts continued

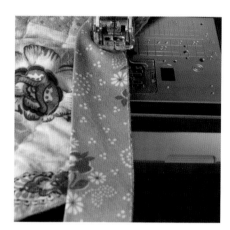

18 Realign the raw edge of the binding with the raw edge of the quilt and lower the presser foot. Continue stitching. Repeat this at each inside corner as you sew the binding to the quilt.

19 Stop sewing when you reach the peak before the beginning stitches. Align the raw edges of the binding and quilt. When you reach the end of the angled edge fold and crease the binding to match.

20 Trim the excess binding leaving a generous 1/4".

21 Insert the extra 1/4" into the angled edge and continue stitching to secure in place.

22 Turn the quilt over and fold the binding to the back, covering the raw edges. Hold the binding in place with pins. Use an appliqué or slipstitch to sew the binding to the quilt back, covering the stitching line.

Miter each peak and inside corner as you come to it, stitching so the bulk on the front and back of the quilt is going in opposite directions.

Quilting Designs for Hexagon Quilts

Hexagon quilts can be quilted in nearly as many ways as they can be designed. This section will serve as a quilting resource for your hexagon projects. Quilting designs are suggested for each project in the book, but feel free to experiment. The designs can be hand or machine quilted.

Outline Quilting

Hexagon quilts are often outline quilted 1/4"
away from the seam around each shape.
Experiment with using thick threads and hand
quilting big stitches 1/2" – 1" away from each
seam. This simple change will give your quilt a
very different look.

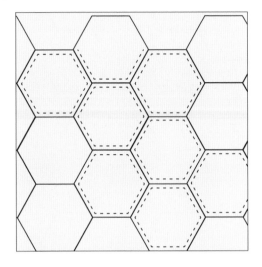

Amish waves/Elbow Quilting

Use a template or quarter circle to create this
design. Beginning in the corner of the quilt, mark
the first quarter circle. After the quarter circle is
drawn, continue to echo it until you are happy
with the design. Continue repeating the design in
the same manner.

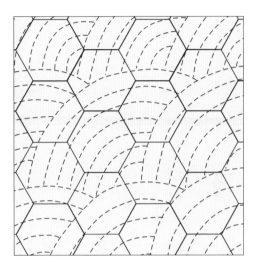

Triangles

Use the center point on the straight side
of each hexagon to draft triangle designs
within each shape.

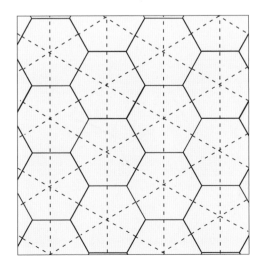

45-degree Crosshatch

Mark 45-degree diagonal lines of quilting
approximately every 2" one way across the
quilt top. Repeat the diagonal lines going in the
opposite direction to create a crosshatch design.

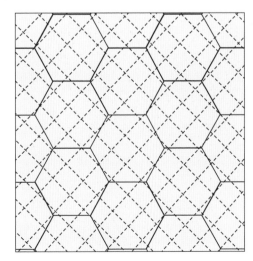

Wavy Line 1 Quilting

The wavy line is a modified version of outline quilting. The quilting line is continuous but does not use every seam as a guideline. The line is horizontal and marked 1/2" away from the seam. It can be machine quilted with a walking foot or free motion quilted.

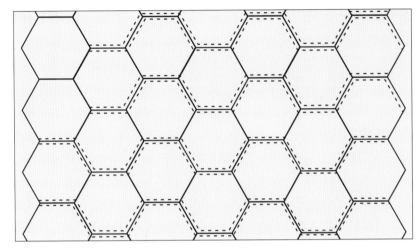

Wavy Line 2 Quilting

This quilting design is the same as Wavy Line 1, but the lines are marked vertically instead of horizontally.

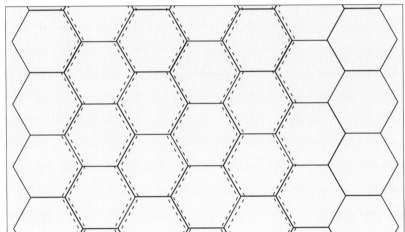

Cubes 1
Echo the diamond for an interesting design on a cube quilt.

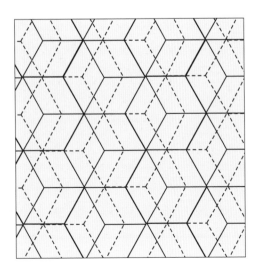

Cubes 2
Draft a cube design within each hexagon using every other hexagon point as a guide.

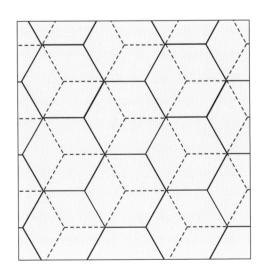

Stripes 1

Quilt vertical lines using the points of the hexagons as a guide.

Stripes 2

This quilting design is the same as Stripes 1, but an additional vertical line of quilting is added through the center of each hexagon. This provides the same density of quilting all over the quilt.

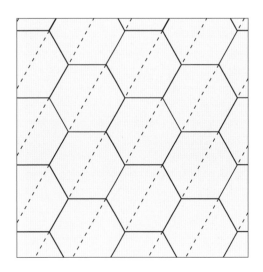

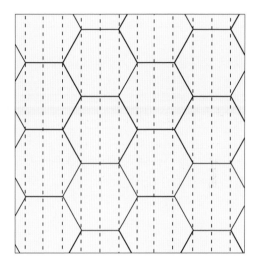

Stripes 3

Mark a diagonal line of quilting through the center of each hexagon and along the seam lines.

Stripes 4

This design is a denser version of Stripes 3. An additional diagonal line of quilting is stitched on either side of the center stitch line.

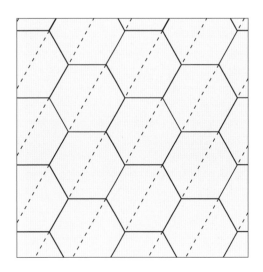

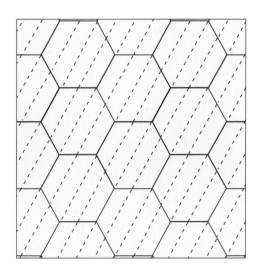

Diamonds 1

Use the center point on opposite straight sides of the hexagon to draft this large diamond design.

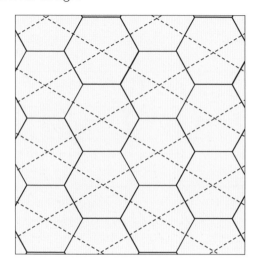

Diamonds 2

Stitching 1/2" away from selected seams in the quilt creates this diamond quilting design.

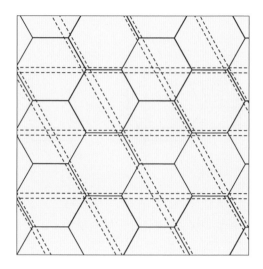

Diamonds 3

Use the center point on each side of the hexagon shapes to create an allover diamond design.

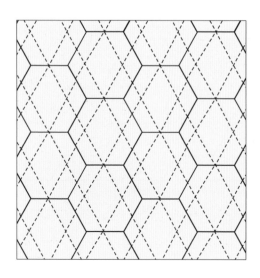

Diamonds 4

Stitch horizontal and diagonal lines 1-3/4" from the seam lines.

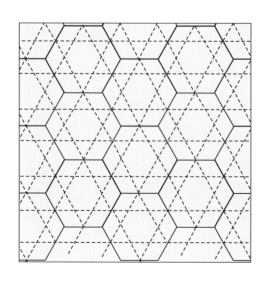

In the Ditch Diamonds

Quilt diagonal lines using the points of the hexagons as a guide.

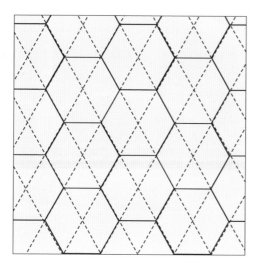

Circles 1

Mark hexagon points and connect them using a compass to create circles. Refer to Drafting Hexagon Shapes on page 9.

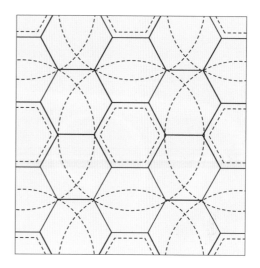

Circles 2

This design is a version of Circles 1 with the circles surrounding the individual hexagons.

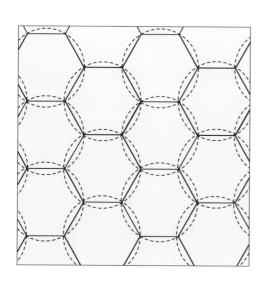

Tying knots

Tie reef or square knots in the center of each hexagon and at each point.

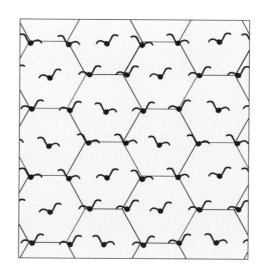

The Projects

You will find a wide array of projects in this section—from simple to a bit more challenging. All the projects may be hand or machine pieced, or if you prefer, combine the two techniques within one project. Hexagons are created using diamond, kite and triangle shapes or a combination of these shapes. Read through Hexagon Basics beginning on page 8 before starting the projects.

Hexagon Table Runner

Finished Table Runner Size: 35" x 8-1/2"

Begin your hexagon journey with this fun and easy table runner. Use one fabric for the hexagons or choose an assortment. Since this project is simply sewing a row of hexagons together it can be as long or short as you wish. The featured project uses five hexagons.

Fabric Requirements

1/2 yard (.5m) assorted light print fabric for hexagons

Note: For a scrappier look, use (5) 10" assorted fabric squares.

12" x 40" backing fabric

1/2 yard (.5m) binding fabric

12" x 40" batting

- -

Fabric quantities are based on 40" usable width of fabric. Sew with a 1/4" seam allowance unless otherwise noted. wof = width of fabric

Refer to Hexagon Basics on pages 8-63 before beginning the project.

Cutting

From light print fabric, cut:
  5 hexagons using the template on page 25.

From binding fabric, cut:
  2-1/2" bias strips to equal approximately 100".

Method

1. Lay out the hexagons in a single row.

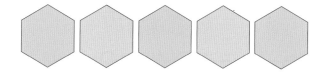

2. Layer two hexagons, right sides together. Using the holes in the template, mark the 1/4" seams on the wrong side of the top hexagon.

Note: Since the hexagon seam allowances are not sewn through, I use a shorter stitch length to keep the stitches from pulling apart. A shorter stitch length also gives me more control over the accuracy of the stitches.

Hexagon Table Runner continued

3. Stitch the hexagons together along one edge, starting and stopping at the 1/4" seam marks. Leave approximately 2" of thread at the stopping mark. Remove the hexagons from the machine. Press the seams open.

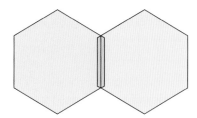

Note: By leaving a few inches of extra thread at the end, the stitches will not come undone if they are pulled. I prefer to do this rather than making securing stitches since this often adds bulk to the seam and doesn't allow flexibility when setting in the hexagons. If you need extra insurance, stitch one stitch past the marks at each end.

4. Continue to sew the remaining hexagons together in the same manner to complete the row.

5. Layer the table runner top, batting and backing together. Baste the layers together using your favorite basting technique. Since this was a small project I used 505® Spray and Fix.

6. Quilt as desired. The table runner shown was quilted using long lines of zigzag stitches approximately 1/2" apart. Refer to pages 64-69 for more quilting ideas.

7. Trim the backing and batting even with the runner top.

8. Sew the bias binding strips together on the diagonal to make one long continuous strip. Press the strip in half, wrong sides together, along the length.

9. Sew the bias binding to the table runner referring to pages 59-63.

Hexagon Table Runner
Finished Table Runner Size: 35" x 8-1/2"

Granny Mat

Finished Mat Size: 21-1/4" x 20-1/4"

Build your skills by making this small granny mat. Although it is a classic flower shape, the hexagons are sewn together in rows, making it even easier to stitch.

Fabric Requirements

10" print fabric square for center hexagon

1/2 yard (.5m) print fabric or (2) 1/4 yard (.25m) assorted print fabrics for outer hexagons
  Note: The project shown uses two different fabrics.

3/4 yard (.7m) backing fabric

1/2 yard (.5m) binding fabric

25" x 25" batting

- -

Fabric quantities are based on 40" usable width of fabric. Sew with a 1/4" seam allowance unless otherwise noted. wof = width of fabric

Refer to Hexagon Basics on pages 8-63 before beginning the project.

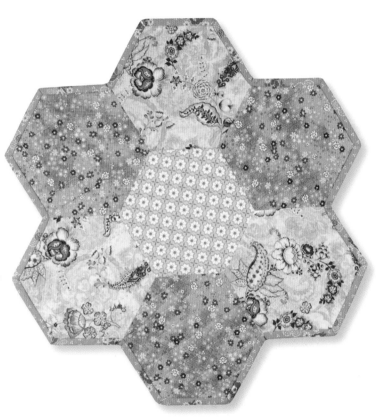

Cutting

From 10" print fabric square, cut:
  (1) center hexagon using the template on page 25.

From print fabric, cut:
  (2) 7-1/2" strips. From each strip, cut: (3) outer hexagons using the template on page 25.

From backing fabric, cut:
  25" square

From binding fabric, cut:
  2-1/2" bias strips to equal approximately 80".

Granny Mat continued

Method

1. Using the holes in the template, mark the 1/4" seams on the wrong side of the hexagons.

2. Lay out the hexagons in vertical rows as shown.

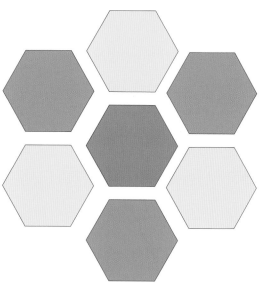

3. Working with one row at a time, layer the hexagons right sides together. Stitch the hexagons together along one edge, starting and stopping at the 1/4" seam mark. Do not sew through the seam allowance. Press the seams open.

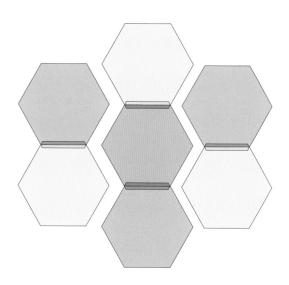

Granny Mat continued

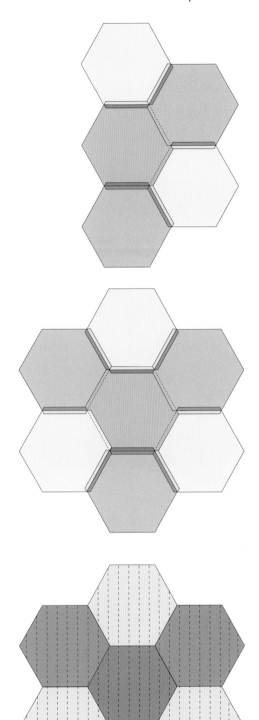

4. Referring to Machine Sewing Hexagons on pages 38-41, sew an outside row of hexagons to the center row. Remember to start and stop sewing at the 1/4" marks.

5. Press the outside edge seams open. Press the other seams in alternating directions.

6. Sew the remaining outside row to the center row in the same manner.

7. Layer the mat top, batting and backing together. Baste the layers together using your favorite basting technique. Since this was a small project I used 505® Spray and Fix.

8. Quilt as desired. The mat shown was hand quilted with straight lines in a big stitch. Refer to pages 64-69 for more quilting ideas.

9. Trim the backing and batting even with the mat top.

10. Sew the bias binding strips together on the diagonal to make one long continuous strip. Press the strip in half, wrong sides together, along the length.

11. Sew the bias binding on the mat referring to pages 59-63.

Pincushions & Coasters

Finished Pincushion or Coaster Size: 7-1/2" at widest point

The coasters and pincushions began as a way to test fabrics, shapes and layout designs. They soon became favorite gifts and useful items to have on hand. These small projects are great fun when you don't have time to tackle a whole quilt.

Pincushion

Fabric Requirements

Note: The fabric requirements listed are for the featured pincushion. Refer to page 80 for additional layout designs.

(1) 4" x 9-1/2" light print fabric strip for triangles

(1) 4" x 9-1/2" medium-to-dark print fabric strip for triangles

(1) 10" square backing fabric

Poly-Fil® or similar stuffing material

Button for pincushion center

Strong thread to attach button

Cutting

From light print fabric strip, cut:
(3) triangles using the template on page 22.

From medium-to-dark print fabric strip, cut:
(3) triangles using the template on page 22.

From backing fabric, cut:
(1) hexagon using the template on page 25.

Pincushions & Coasters continued

Method

1. Sew the triangles together along the long edges to make a hexagon.

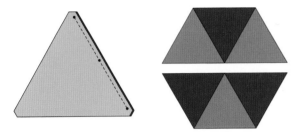

2. Using a small stitch setting, sew a row of reinforcing stitches along one straight of grain edge on the front hexagon. Repeat on the hexagon backing shape.

3. Layer the hexagon shapes right sides together. Begin sewing the shapes together on the side with the reinforced stitches. Overlap one end of the reinforced stitches slightly. Continue sewing around the hexagons, stitching across the corners with two stitches for a better finish.

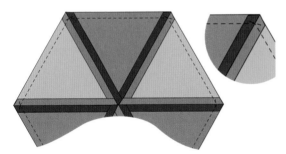

4. To finish, slightly overlap the other end of reinforced stitches and secure the threads. Leave a 1-1/2" opening for stuffing.

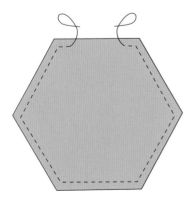

5. Trim away any excess fabric at each corner. Turn the hexagon right sides out, poking out the corners. Stuff the hexagon with Poly-Fil® and slipstitch the opening closed along the line of reinforced stitches.

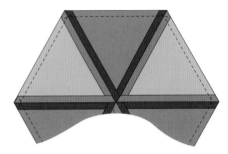

6. Using a strong thread, sew a button on the front of the pincushion, stitching through to the back and pulling the thread tight as you work. Secure the thread to finish.

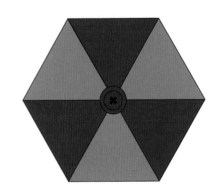

Pincushions & Coasters continued

Coasters

Fabric Requirements

(3) 4" x 8" assorted scraps of coordinating fabric for diamonds

(1) 10" square backing fabric

(1) 10" square batting

Cutting

From assorted scraps, cut:

(3) diamonds using the template on page 23.

Method

1. Referring to Machine Sewing Hexagons on pages 38-41, sew the three diamonds together to form a hexagon.

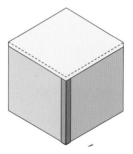

2. Using a small stitch setting, sew a row of reinforcing stitches along one straight of grain edge on the hexagon shape along the 1/4" seam allowance line.

Pincushions & Coasters continued

3. Layer the hexagon shape and backing square right sides together. With the backing square on the bottom, lay the pieces on the batting.

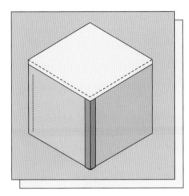

4. Begin sewing the layers together on the side with the reinforced stitches. Overlap one end of the reinforced stitches slightly. Continue sewing, stitching across the corners with two stitches for a better finish.

5. To finish, overlap the other end of reinforced stitches slightly and secure the threads. Leave a 1-1/2" opening for turning.

6. Trim the batting close to the seam line.

7. Trim the backing fabric even with the top hexagon. Trim any excess fabric at the corners.

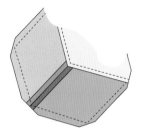

8. Turn the hexagons right side out, poking out the corners. Slipstitch the opening closed.

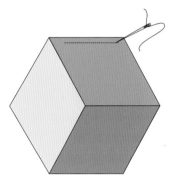

9. Outline quilt 1/4" from the seams around the diamond shapes.

Hexagon Honeycomb Quilt

Finished Quilt Size: 72-1/2" x 75"

The wide assortment of fabrics in this quilt will make a serious dent in your stash. The different scale of prints makes it interesting and keeps the eye wandering to see what else there is to discover. This quilt was sewn together in rows with minimal thought to placement.

Fabric Requirements

6-2/3 yards (5.5m) assorted selection of coordinating fabrics for hexagons

Note: You may also use 30 fat quarters and (3) 4" x wof strips for the hexagons.

4-5/8 yards (4.25m) backing fabric

1 yard (1m) binding fabric

83" x 85" batting

- -

Fabric quantities are based on 40" usable width of fabric. Sew with a 1/4" seam allowance unless otherwise noted. wof = width of fabric

Refer to Hexagon Basics on pages 8-63 before beginning the project.

Cutting

Note: Use the holes in the templates to mark the 1/4" seam on the wrong side of the hexagons and half hexagons.

From assorted coordinating fabrics, cut:
 120 hexagons using the template on page 25.
 12 half hexagons using the template on page 25.

From backing fabric, cut:
 (2) equal lengths, removing the selvages.

From binding fabric, cut:
 2-1/2" bias strips to equal approximately 260".

Hexagon Honeycomb Quilt continued

Method

1. Referring to the diagram, lay out the hexagons in 12 vertical rows with 10 hexagons and 1 half hexagon in each row.

    Note: The half hexagons will alternate between the top and bottom of each row.

2. Sew the hexagons, right sides together, in rows. Start and stop sewing at the 1/4" marks on the wrong side of the hexagons. Press all seams open.

3. Sew the rows together pivoting at the 1/4" marks to set in each hexagon. Refer to Machine Sewing Hexagons on pages 38-41 for more information. Sew through the seam allowances at the top and bottom of the quilt.

    Note: When sewing the rows together I find it helps to have one row draped over my shoulder as I feed them into the sewing machine. This keeps the rows from getting bunched up as they are fed under the presser foot.

4. As the rows are sewn together, press them in alternating directions.

    Note: It is not necessary to press the seams open since the top and bottom of the quilt are straight edges. You have already pressed the side seams open.

5. Sew the 2 backing pieces, right sides together, along one long edge using a 1/2" seam allowance. Press the seam open.

6. Layer the backing, batting and quilt top together. Baste the layers together using your favorite basting technique.

7. Quilt as desired. The Hexagon Honeycomb quilt was machine quilted with the Amish Waves pattern. Refer to pages 64-69 for more ideas on quilting hexagon quilts.

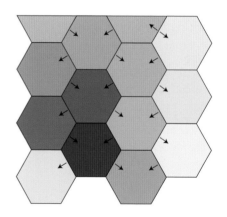

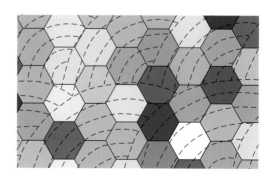

Hexagon Honeycomb Quilt continued

8. Trim the backing and batting even with the quilt top.

9. Sew the bias binding strips together on the diagonal to make one long continuous strip.

Press the strip in half, wrong sides together, along the length.

10. Sew the bias binding to the quilt referring to pages 59-63.

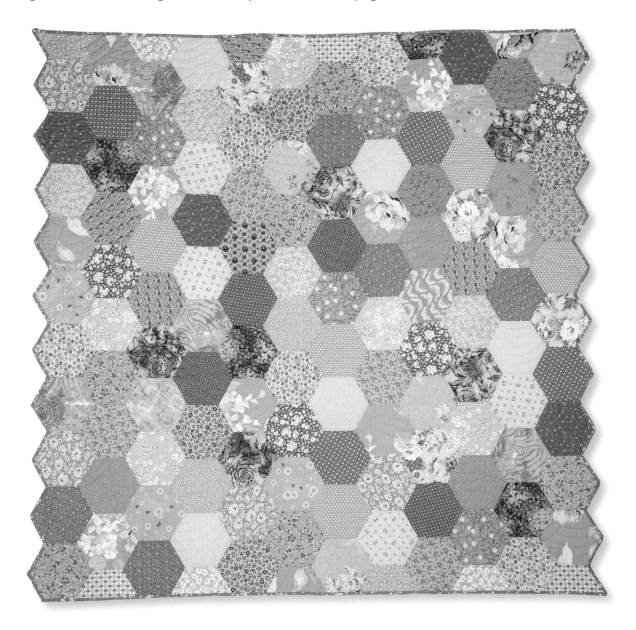

Hexagon Honeycomb Quilt
Finished Quilt Size: 72-1/2" x 75"

Grandmother's Flower Garden Quilt

Finished Quilt Size: 56" x 78"

This classic quilt takes on a contemporary twist with large-scale hexagons creating big bold flowers. For a different look, use a variety of fabrics in the same color value for the background rather than just one fabric as in the featured quilt.

Fabric Requirements

3 yards (2.75m) light gray print fabric for background

(14) assorted purple fat quarters for flower petals

(7) assorted purple 10" squares for flower centers

3-3/4 yards (3.4m) backing fabric

1-1/2 yards (1.5m) binding fabric

66" x 88" batting

- -

Fabric quantities are based on 40" usable width of fabric. Sew with a 1/4" seam allowance unless otherwise noted. wof = width of fabric

Refer to Hexagon Basics on pages 8-63 before beginning the project.

Cutting

Note: Use the holes in the templates to mark the 1/4" seam on the wrong side of the hexagons.

From light gray print fabric, cut:
50 hexagons using the template on page 25.
8 half hexagons using the template on page 25.

From assorted purple fat quarters, cut:
42 hexagons using the template on page 25.
You will only use 38.

From assorted purple 10" squares, cut:
7 hexagons using the template on page 25.

From backing fabric, cut:
(2) equal lengths, removing the selvages.

From binding fabric, cut:
2-1/2" bias strips to equal approximately 350".

Method

1. Referring to the Quilt Top Assembly Diagram, on page 88, lay out the hexagons and half hexagons in 9 vertical rows as shown. Pay careful attention to the color placement. The purple hexagons should form flowers when the rows are sewn together. Each odd row has 11 hexagons and each even row has 10 hexagons and 2 half hexagons.

Grandmother's Flower Garden Quilt continued

Note: Place the hexagons at the top and bottom of the quilt with the straight of grain on the outside edge for added stability.

2. Sew the hexagons, right sides together, in rows. Start and stop sewing at the 1/4" marks on the wrong side of the hexagons. Press all seams open.

3. Sew the rows together pivoting at the 1/4" marks to set in each hexagon. Refer to Sewing Hexagons by Machine on pages 38-41 for more information. Sew through the seam allowances at the top and bottom of the quilt.

Note: When sewing the rows together I find it helps to have one row draped over my shoulder as I feed them into the sewing machine. This keeps the rows from getting bunched up as they are fed under the presser foot.

4. Press the seams in each row in alternating directions.

5. Sew the 2 backing pieces, right sides together, along one long edge using a 1/2" seam allowance. Press the seam open.

6. Layer the backing, batting and quilt top together. Baste the layers together using your favorite basting technique.

7. Quilt as desired. The Grandmother's Flower Garden quilt was hand quilted with elbow quilting. Place your elbow in the bottom right corner of the quilt. If you are left handed, place your elbow in the bottom left corner of the quilt. With a marking chalk draw an arc using your elbow as the pivot. Quilt the drawn line.

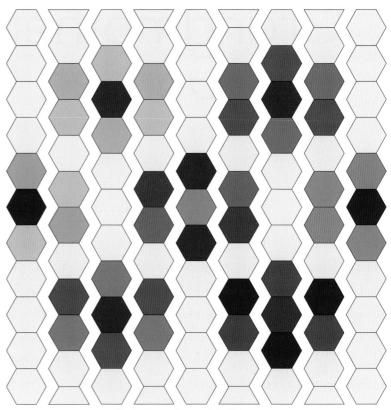

Quilt Top Assembly Diagram

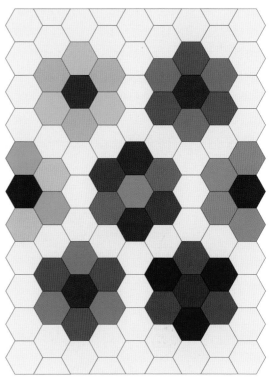

Grandmother's Flower Garden Quilt continued

8. Fill in with subsequent arcs spacing them roughly a needle length apart. Quilt around the outside edge of the quilt and then fill in the center. Refer to pages 64-69 for more quilting ideas.

9. Trim the backing and batting even with the quilt top.

10. Sew the bias binding strips together on the diagonal to make one long continuous strip. Press the strip in half, wrong sides together, along the length.

11. Sew the bias binding to the quilt referring to pages 59-63.

Grandmother's Flower Garden Quilt
Finished Quilt Size: 56" x 78"

Hexagon Flower Garden Honeycomb Quilt

Finished Quilt Size: 95" x 91"

This quilt provides the perfect setting for your favorite fabrics. While the layout and planning takes a bit of time, the quilt sews up quickly in rows. Use contrasting fabrics so the flowers won't blend together. You will need extra hexagons to fill in the spaces between the flowers. Choose a fabric that recedes into the background.

If laying out all those hexagons seems daunting, but you don't mind sewing inset seams, make all the hexagon flowers first. Lay them out, insert the filler hexagons and then sew the quilt top together.

Fabric Requirements

(25) assorted 10" squares for flower centers

(23) assorted 1/2 yard (.5m) fabrics for flower petals

7/8 yard (.8m) fabric for filler hexagons

8-1/2 yards (7.75m) backing fabric

1 yard (1m) binding fabric

105" x 101" batting

Fabric quantities are based on 40" usable width of fabric. Sew with a 1/4" seam allowance unless otherwise noted. wof = width of fabric

Refer to Hexagon Basics on pages 8-63 before beginning the project.

Cutting

Note: Use the holes in the templates to mark the 1/4" seam on the wrong side of the hexagons.

From each assorted 10" fabric square, cut:
    1 hexagon using the template on page 25.

From assorted 1/2 yard fabrics, cut:
    153 hexagons using the template on page 25.
    17 half hexagons using the template on page 25.

From filler fabric, cut:
    15 hexagons using the template on page 25.

From binding fabric, cut:
    2-1/2" bias strips to equal approximately 420".

Hexagon Flower Garden Honeycomb Quilt continued

Method

1. Referring to the diagram, lay out the hexagons in 15 vertical rows with 13 hexagons and 1 half hexagon in each row.

Note: The half hexagons will alternate between the top and bottom of each row.

2. Sew the hexagons, right sides together, in rows. Start and stop sewing at the 1/4" marks on the wrong side of the hexagons. Press all seams open.

3. Sew the rows together pivoting at the 1/4" marks to set in each hexagon. Refer to Machine Sewing Hexagons on pages 38-41 for more information. Sew through the seam allowances at the top and bottom of the quilt.

Note: When sewing the rows together I find it helps to have one row draped over my shoulder as I feed them into the sewing machine. This keeps the rows from getting bunched up as they are fed under the presser foot.

4. As the rows are sewn together, press them in alternating directions.

5. Layer the backing, batting and quilt top together. Baste the layers together using your favorite basting technique.

6. Quilt as desired. The Flower Garden Honeycomb quilt was machine quilted with a hanging diamond design. The diamonds were drawn at 90-degrees with a ruler and Hera Marker. Refer to pages 64-69 for more ideas on quilting hexagon quilts.

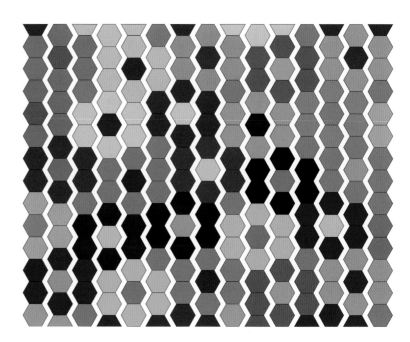

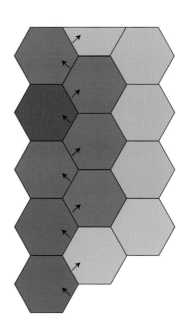

Hexagon Flower Garden Honeycomb Quilt continued

7. Trim the backing and batting even with the quilt top.

8. Sew the bias binding strips together on the diagonal to make one long continuous strip.

Press the strip in half, wrong sides together, along the length.

9. Sew the bias binding to the quilt referring to pages 59-63.

Hexagon Flower Garden Honeycomb Quilt

Finished Quilt Size: 95" x 91"

Sometime Stars Quilt

Finished Quilt Size: 72" x 91"

I love the way the stars in this quilt come and go depending on where you focus your eye. This versatile pattern allows you to use fabrics from your stash for a scrappy look or choose a favorite color as the focal point. For the featured quilt I had lots of lilac scraps to show off so I used it in the hexagons. In the color option quilts (page 99) I used colored fabrics for the triangles to create a different look. You can also group the same value color fabrics around one of the hexagons to emphasize the star design.

Fabric Requirements

5-7/8 yards (5.4m) assorted lilac fabric for hexagons

Note: For a scrappier look, use (28) fat quarters or (111) 10" squares.

2 yards (1.75m) light print fabric for triangles

5-5/8 yards (5.2m) backing fabric

1-1/4 yards (1.25m) binding fabric

82" x 101" batting

- -

Fabric quantities are based on 40" usable width of fabric. Sew with a 1/4" seam allowance unless otherwise noted. wof = width of fabric

Refer to Hexagon Basics on pages 8-63 before beginning the project.

Cutting

From assorted lilac fabric, cut:
111 hexagons using the template on page 25.

From light print fabric, cut:
(17) 4" x wof strips. From the strips, cut:
220 triangles using the template on page 24.

From backing fabric, cut:
(2) equal lengths, removing the selvages.

From binding fabric, cut:
2-1/2" bias strips to equal approximately 370".

Sometime Stars Quilt continued

Method

1. Lay out the hexagons and triangles in 13 horizontal rows as shown. The odd-numbered rows (rows A) begin and end with hexagons and have 9 hexagons in each row. The even-numbered rows (rows B) begin and end with triangles and have 8 hexagons in each row.

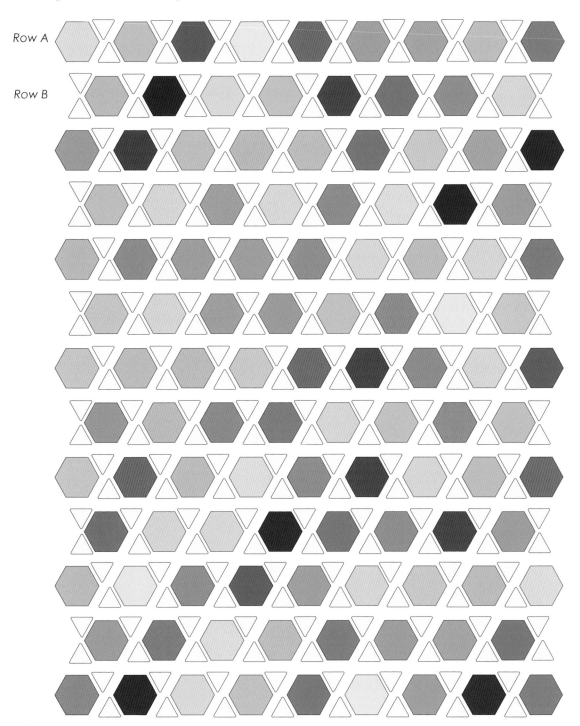

Row A

Row B

Sometime Stars Quilt continued

2. Beginning with rows A, sew the triangles to the hexagons as shown. Press the seams open. The first and last hexagon in each row will have one triangle while the rest will have two.

3. Referring to the diagram, lay two hexagon/triangle units wrong sides together matching the seams. Pin in place where the seams match if you wish. Sew the units together. Press the seams open.

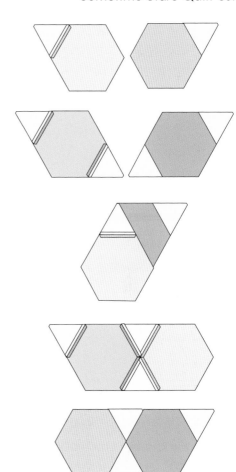

4. Continue sewing the units within each row together until all A rows are complete.

5. For rows B, sew the triangles to the hexagons in the same manner as for rows A. Press the seams open.

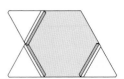

6. Sew the remaining triangle on the end of each row B to the triangle/hexagon unit. Begin sewing at the outside edge and continue to sew through to the seam allowance of the next triangle.

7. Press the seam open.

Sometime Stars Quilt continued

8. Referring to the diagram, lay two triangle/hexagon units wrong sides together matching the seams. Pin in place where the seams match if you wish. Sew the units together. Press the seams open.

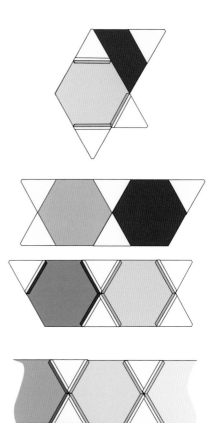

9. Continue sewing the units together within each row until all B rows are complete.

10. Sew the rows together using pins to match the seam lines. Press all seams open to complete the quilt top.

11. Sew the 2 backing pieces, right sides together, along one long edge using a 1/2" seam allowance. Press the seam open.

12. Layer the backing, batting and quilt top together. Baste the layers together using your favorite basting technique.

13. Quilt as desired. The Sometime Stars quilt was machine quilted in an allover vermicelli design. Refer to pages 64-69 for more ideas on quilting hexagon quilts.

14. Trim the backing and batting even with the quilt top.

15. Sew the bias binding strips together on the diagonal to make one long continuous strip.
Press the strip in half, wrong sides together, along the length.

16. Sew the bias binding to the quilt referring to pages 59-63.

Sometime Stars Quilt continued

Sometime Stars Quilt

Finished Quilt Size: 72" x 91"

Color Options

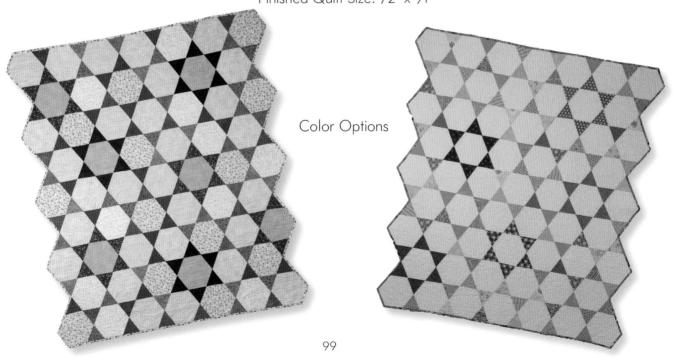

Zigzag Diamonds Quilt

Finished Quilt Size: 70" x 86"

I love the way diamonds zigzag up and down this quilt. Bright, bold, large-scale prints were used to create chains of diamonds while a light print provides contrast in the background.

Fabric Requirements

2-1/3 yards (2m) light/cream fabric for diamonds

3-2/3 yards (3.4m) assorted medium prints for diamonds

Note: You may also use 17 assorted medium print fat quarters for the diamonds.

1-1/3 yards dark print for half diamonds, half hexagons and binding

5-1/3 yards (5m) backing fabric

80" x 96" batting

- -

Fabric quantities are based on 40" usable width of fabric. Sew with a 1/4" seam allowance unless otherwise noted. wof = width of fabric

Refer to Hexagon Basics on pages 8-63 before beginning the project.

Cutting

Note: Use the holes in the templates to mark the 1/4" seam on the wrong side of the diamonds, half diamonds and half hexagons.

From light/cream fabrics, cut:
  145 diamonds using the template on page 23.

From assorted medium print fabrics, cut:
  264 diamonds using the template on page 23.

From dark print fabric, cut:
  11 half hexagons using the template on page 25.
  26 half diamonds using the template on page 23.
  (8) 2-1/2" x wof strips for binding.

From backing fabric, cut:
  (2) equal lengths, removing the selvages.

Method

1. Lay out two medium print diamonds and one light/cream diamond as shown.

2. Layer the two medium print diamonds, right sides together, and begin sewing at the raw edge of the narrow point. Stitch toward the wider angle, stopping at the 1/4" mark on the opposite edge. Press the seam open.

Zigzag Diamonds Quilt continued

3. With right sides together, place the light/cream diamond on the sewn diamonds in step 2, matching raw edges. With the light/cream diamond on the bottom, sew from the raw outer fabric edge to the 1/4" mark above the open seam.

4. Leaving the needle in the work, lift the presser foot and pivot the top piece so it aligns with

the raw edge of the diamond underneath. Lower the presser foot and continue to stitch to the end of the seam. Press seams in one direction. Repeat the steps to make 132 hexagons.

Note: When you pivot the diamonds, tug the top pieces backward so as not to create a pleat in the seam.

5. Referring to the diagram, lay out the hexagons in 11 vertical rows with 12 hexagons in each row.

Note: The half hexagons will alternate between the top and bottom of each row.

Zigzag Diamonds Quilt continued

6. Sew the hexagons, right sides together, in rows. Start and stop sewing at the 1/4" marks on the wrong side of the hexagons. Press all seams open.

Note: In some instances, the 1/4" mark is under the pressed seam.

7. Sew the rows together pivoting at the 1/4" marks to set in each hexagon. Refer to Machine Sewing Hexagons on pages 38-41 for more information. Sew through the seam allowances at the top and bottom of the quilt.

Note: When sewing the rows together I find it helps to have one row draped over my shoulder as I feed them into the sewing machine. This keeps the rows from getting bunched up as they are fed under the presser foot.

8. As the rows are sewn together, press them in alternating directions.

Note: It is not necessary to press the seams open since the top and bottom of the quilt are straight edges and the side seams are already pressed open.

9. Referring to Straightening Hexagon Quilt Edges with Inserts on pages 50-52, set in the half diamonds on the right edge of the quilt top.

Zigzag Diamonds Quilt continued

10. To straighten the left side of the quilt top, sew the half diamonds to the remaining light/cream diamonds from raw edge to raw edge. Press the seams open to make a unit. Make 13 units.

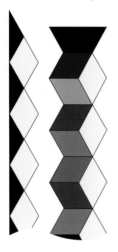

11. Sew the units together as shown to make a row. Sew the pieced row to the left side of the quilt top. Press seams toward the quilt top.

12. Trim the added row even with the quilt top and bottom.

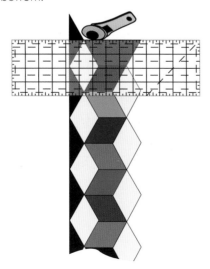

13. Sew the 2 backing pieces, right sides together, along one long edge using a 1/2" seam allowance. Press the seam open.

14. Layer the backing, batting and quilt top together. Baste the layers together using your favorite basting technique.

15. Quilt as desired. The Zigzag Diamonds quilt was quilted with the Amish Waves pattern. Refer to pages 64-69 for more ideas on quilting hexagon quilts.

Note: I started the design in the bottom right corner and worked in rows moving up to the top of the quilt. It doesn't matter if the design runs off the quilt. If you are left-handed, begin the design in the left hand corner.

16. Trim the backing and batting even with the quilt top.

17. Sew the binding strips together on the diagonal to make one long continuous strip. Press the strip in half, wrong sides together, along the length.

18. Sew the binding to the quilt referring to pages 59-63.

Zigzag Diamonds Quilt
Finished Quilt Size: 70" x 86"

Strippy Hexagons and Diamonds Quilt

Finished Quilt Size: 70" x 78"

This quilt was inspired by an antique Durham quilt made in lilac and white solids. I decided to recreate it by adding prints to the design. A large-scale print in colors pulled from the hexagons was used for the diamonds. To add more contrast use only two fabrics—one for the diamonds and one for the hexagons.

Fabric Requirements

5-2/3 yards (4.8m) total of assorted print fabrics for hexagons

Note: You may also use (25) assorted print fat quarters for the hexagons.

1-1/2 yards (1.35m) large-scale print for diamonds and triangles

4-1/2 yards (4.1m) backing fabric

1 yard (1m) binding fabric

80" x 88" batting

- -

Fabric quantities are based on 40" usable width of fabric. Sew with a 1/4" seam allowance unless otherwise noted. wof = width of fabric

Refer to Hexagon Basics on pages 8-63 before beginning the project.

Cutting

Note: Use the holes in the templates to mark the 1/4" seam on the wrong side of the hexagons, diamonds and triangles.

From assorted print fabrics, cut:
100 hexagons using the template on page 25.

From large-scale print, cut:
81 diamonds using the template on page 23.
18 triangles using the template on page 24.

From backing fabric, cut:
(2) equal lengths, removing the selvages.

From binding fabric, cut:
2-1/2" bias strips to equal approximately 320".

Strippy Hexagons and Diamonds Quilt continued

Method

1. Referring to the diagram, lay out the hexagons in 10 vertical rows with 10 hexagons in each row.

2. Sew the hexagons, right sides together, in rows. Start and stop sewing at the 1/4" marks on the wrong side of the hexagons. Press all seams open. Set row 10 aside.

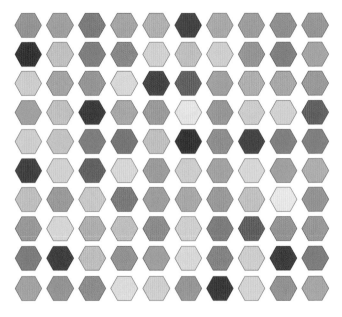

3. With right sides together, place a triangle on the top hexagon in row 1 as shown. Sew from the raw outer fabric edge to the 1/4" mark on the triangle. Press the seam open.

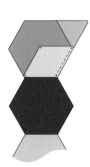

4. With right sides together, place a diamond on the hexagon, aligning the raw edges and overlapping the triangle's 1/4" mark. Stitch the diamond to the hexagon, starting and stopping at the 1/4" marks.

5. Leaving the needle in the work, lift the presser foot and pivot the diamond so it aligns with the raw edge of the hexagon underneath. Lower the presser foot and continue to stitch to the next 1/4" mark. Press seams open.

Note: When you pivot the diamond, tug the top piece backward slightly so as not to create a pleat in the seam.

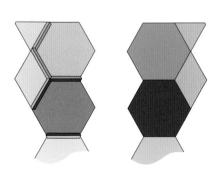

Strippy Hexagons and Diamonds Quilt continued

6. Working down the row, set in the next 8 diamonds and 1 triangle in the same manner. Press the seams open after each addition.

7. Referring to steps 3-6, stitch triangles and diamonds to the next 8 hexagon rows. You should have 9 hexagon/triangle/diamond rows.

8. Sew the rows together pivoting at the 1/4" marks to set in each piece. Refer to Machine Sewing Hexagons on page 38-41 for more information. Sew through the seam allowances at the top and bottom of the quilt. Press the seams in alternating directions.

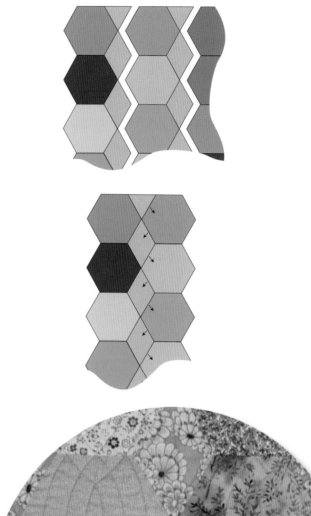

9. Sew the remaining row of hexagons to the right edge of the quilt top.

10. Sew the 2 backing pieces, right sides together, along one long edge using a 1/2" seam allowance. Press the seam open.

11. Layer the backing, batting and quilt top together. Baste the layers together using your favorite basting technique.

12. Quilt as desired. The Strippy Hexagons and Diamonds quilt was quilted using the patterns on pages 110-111. Refer to pages 64-69 for more ideas on quilting hexagon quilts.

13. Trim the backing and batting even with the quilt top.

14. Sew the bias binding strips together on the diagonal to make one long continuous strip. Press the strip in half, wrong sides together, along the length.

15. Sew the bias binding on the quilt referring to pages 59-63.

Strippy Hexagons and Diamonds Quilt continued

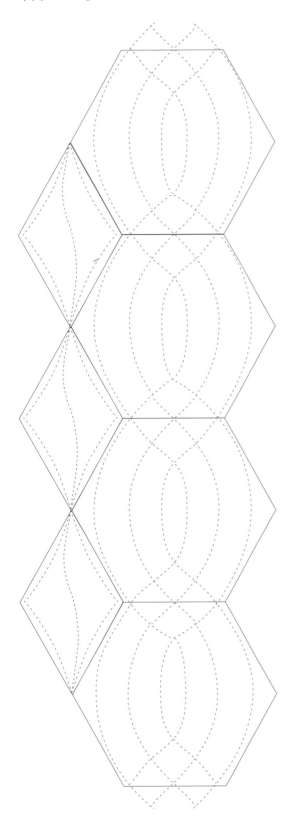

Enlarge 115%

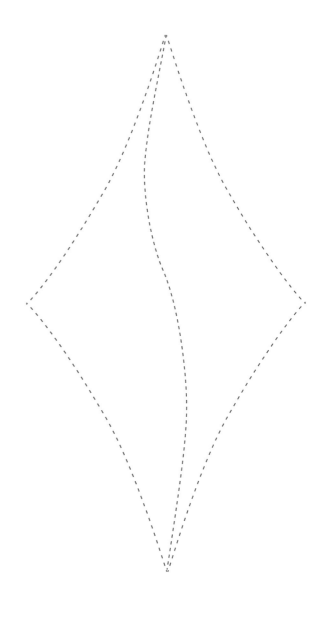

Strippy Hexagons and Diamonds Quilt continued

Enlarge 115%

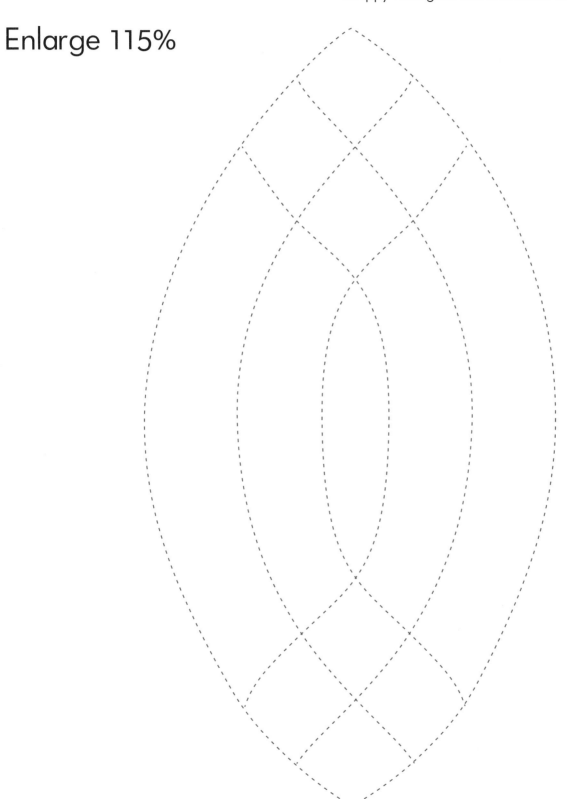

Strippy Hexagons and Diamonds Quilt continued

Strippy Hexagons and Diamonds Quilt
Finished Quilt Size: 70" x 78"

Rose Star One Patch Quilt

Finished Quilt Size: 71-1/2" x 68-1/2"

I love the Rose Star One Patch block. Fussy cutting or using striped fabric in the center makes this quilt a show stopper. While it looks complex, the quilt is created using kite shapes to make the triangles that form the large hexagons. My fading hydrangea flowers inspired the colors in the quilt.

If you don't want to invest time in an entire quilt, one block makes a stunning table topper. It's perfect with Christmas or other seasonal fabric.

Fabric Requirements

(9) assorted 1/4 yard fabrics for block centers

Note: For maximum effect, I used a striped fabric for my block centers. You could also fussy cut the kites for the block centers. To fussy cut, you will need a fabric with 6 pattern repeats.

(9) assorted dark print fat quarters or 1/4 yard fabrics for A kites

(9) assorted medium print fat quarters or 1/4 yard fabrics for B kites

(18) assorted medium to dark print fat quarters or 1/4 yard fabrics for C and D kites

2-1/4 yards (2.10m) assorted light print background fabric

4-1/3 yards (4m) backing fabric

5/8 yard (.6m) binding fabric

81" x 78" batting

Fabric quantities are based on 40" usable width of fabric. Sew with a 1/4" seam allowance unless otherwise noted. wof = width of fabric

Refer to Hexagon Basics on pages 8-63 before beginning the project.

Rose Star One Patch Quilt continued

Cutting

Note: Use the holes in the templates to mark the 1/4" seam on the wrong side of the kites.

From block center fabric, cut:
54 center kites using the template on page 24.

From assorted dark print fabrics, cut:
108 A kites using the template on page 24.

From assorted medium print fabrics, cut:
108 B kites using the template on page 24.

From assorted medium to dark print fabrics, cut:
162 C and D kites using the template on page 24.
Note: You will need 54 C kites and 108 D kites.

From assorted light print background fabrics, cut:
276 background kites using the template on page 24.
24 half kites using the template on page 24.

From backing fabric, cut:
(2) equal lengths, removing the selvages.

From binding fabric, cut:
(8) 2-1/2" x wof strips.

Method

Note: Each hexagon consists of 6 large triangles. The kites create the large triangles. You may wish to lay the kites out in the hexagon shape before you begin sewing.

1. Layer two matching A kite shapes, right sides together, with raw edges aligned. Begin sewing at the outside edge on a straight of grain side. Stop stitching at the 1/4" mark. Press seam open.

2. With right sides together, place a center kite on the sewn kites in step 1, matching raw edges.

3. With the center kite on the bottom, sew from the raw outer fabric edge to the 1/4" mark above the open seam.

4. Leaving the needle in the work, lift the presser foot and pivot the top piece so it aligns with the raw edge of the kite underneath. Lower the presser foot and continue to stitch to the end of the seam. Press seams in opposite directions. Make 9 sets of 6 matching A/Center triangles.

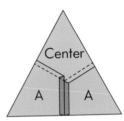

5. Referring to steps 1-4, use B and C kites to make 9 sets of 6 B/C matching triangles. Use D kites and background triangles to make 12 sets of matching D/Background triangles.

6. Place an A/Center triangle and B/C triangle right sides together, matching the center seam. Sew the triangles together as shown. Make 9 sets of 6 matching center units. Within each matching set, press 3 of the center unit in one direction and 3 in the opposite direction.

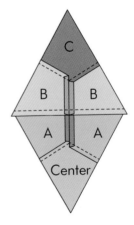

Rose Star One Patch Quilt continued

7. Sew matching D/Background triangles to opposite sides of a center unit as shown. Press seams in opposite directions to make a large triangle. Make 9 sets of 6 matching large triangles.

Note: Make sure you are pressing the seams in the same manner with each triangle.

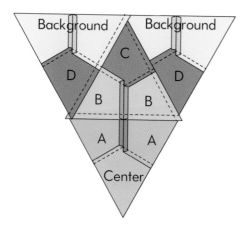

8. Lay out 6 matching large triangles. Sew 3 triangles together to make a half hexagon as shown.

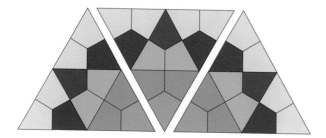

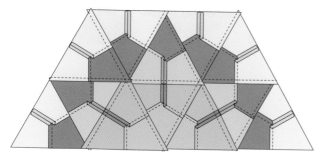

9. Sew the remaining 3 large triangles together to make a half hexagon. Press the seams in the same direction on both. Due to the way the seams have been pressed, the half hexagons should all lock together for a neat finish. Make 18 sets of 2 matching half hexagons. Do not sew the sets together.

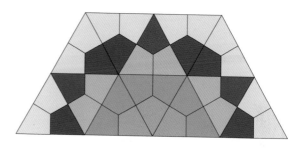

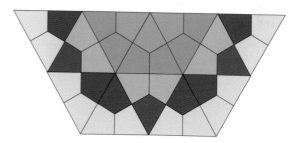

Rose Star One Patch Quilt continued

10. Lay out 5 background kites and 2 half kites as shown. Sew 3 kites together in a triangle, referring to steps 1-4.

11. Sew the triangle and remaining pieces together. Press seams open to make a side triangle. Referring to the diagram, make 6 side triangles and 6 side triangles reversed.

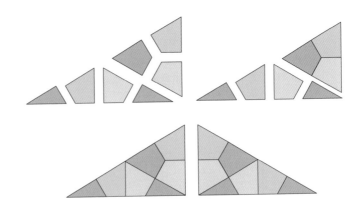

12. Lay out the half hexagons and side triangles in 6 horizontal rows as shown.

13. Sew the side triangles to the half hexagons. Sew the half hexagons together in rows. Press the seams open.

14. Sew the rows together, pressing the seams open to complete the quilt top.

15. Sew the 2 backing pieces, right sides together, along one long edge using a 1/2" seam allowance. Press the seam open.

16. Layer the backing, batting and quilt top together. Baste the layers together using your favorite basting technique.

17. Quilt as desired. The Rose Star One Patch quilt was machine quilted in an allover vermicelli design. Refer to pages 64-69 for more ideas on quilting hexagon quilts.

18. Trim the backing and batting even with the quilt top.

19. Sew the binding strips together on the diagonal to make one long continuous strip. Press the strip in half, wrong sides together, along the length.

20. Sew the binding on the quilt referring to pages 59-63.

Rose Star One Patch Quilt

Finished Quilt Size: 71-1/2" x 68-1/2"

Blueberry Jam Quilt

Finished Quilt Size: 60-1/2" x 69"

Dig deep into your scraps to make this stash buster quilt. You will love the way the shapes come and go depending on where your eyes focus. A large variety of fabrics will equal a more interesting quilt.

Fabric Requirements

4-5/8 yards (4.3m) total assorted fabric scraps
   Note: You may also use 26 fat quarters or
   52 fat eighths.

4 yards (3.6m) backing fabric

1/2 yard (.5m) binding fabric

70" x 79" batting

- -

Fabric quantities are based on 40" usable width of fabric.
Sew with a 1/4" seam allowance unless otherwise noted.
wof = width of fabric

Refer to Hexagon Basics on pages 8-63
before beginning the project.

Cutting

Note: Use the holes in the templates to mark the
   1/4" seam on the wrong side of the kites and
   half kites.

From assorted fabric scraps, cut:
   590 kites using the template on page 24.
   20 half kites using the template on page 24.

From backing fabric, cut:
   (2) equal lengths, removing the selvages.

From binding fabric, cut:
   (7) 2-1/2" x wof strips.

Method

1. Lay out three kite shapes
    as shown.

2. Layer two kite shapes, right sides together, with
    raw edges aligned. Begin sewing at the outside
    edge on a straight of grain side. Stop stitching at
    the 1/4" mark. Press seam open.

3. With right sides together, place the third kite
    shape on the sewn kites in step 2, matching
    raw edges.

4. With the third kite on the bottom, sew from the
    raw outer fabric edge to the 1/4" mark above
    the open seam.

Blueberry Jam Quilt continued

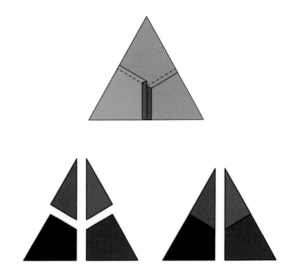

5. Leaving the needle in the work, lift the presser foot and pivot the top piece so it aligns with the raw edge of the kite underneath. Lower the presser foot and continue to stitch to the end of the seam. Press seams in opposite directions. Repeat the steps to make 190 triangles.

6. Lay out a kite and half kite as shown. Stitch the pieces together to make a partial triangle. Press the seam open. Make a total of 10 partial triangles and 10 reverse partial triangles.

7. Lay out the partial triangles and triangles in 10 vertical rows as shown. You will have 5 A rows and 5 B rows. The partial triangles and reverse partial triangles will alternate at the top and bottom of each row.

8. Sew the pieces together in rows, pressing the seams open as you stitch.

9. Sew the rows together alternating rows A and B on the quilt top. Press the seams open.

10. Sew the 2 backing pieces, right sides together, along one long edge using a 1/2" seam allowance. Press the seam open.

11. Layer the backing, batting and quilt top together. Baste the layers together using your favorite basting technique.

12. Quilt as desired. Since the Blueberry Jam quilt is very busy, I machine quilted it in an allover squiggle design. Refer to pages 64-69 for more ideas on quilting hexagon quilts.

13. Trim the backing and batting even with the quilt top.

14. Sew the binding strips together on the diagonal to make one long continuous strip. Press the strip in half, wrong sides together, along the length.

15. Sew the binding on the quilt referring to pages 59-63.

Blueberry Jam Quilt
Finished Quilt Size: 60-1/2" x 69"

Tumbling Stars Quilt

Finished Quilt Size: 64" x 84"

I love the way stars appear after the hexagons are sewn together. The Tumbling Stars quilt is a wonderful way to use scraps or a favorite collection of blending prints. Simply reverse the placement of the light and dark diamonds in the construction for a different design.

Fabric Requirements

3-1/4 yards (3m) light print fabric

Note: You may also use 15 fat quarters or (28) 4" x wof strips.

3-1/4 yards (3m) medium print fabric

Note: You may also use 15 fat quarters or (28) 4" x wof strips.

4-1/8 yards (3.8m) backing fabric

5/8 yard (.6m) binding fabric

94" x 74" batting

- -

Fabric quantities are based on 40" usable width of fabric. Sew with a 1/4" seam allowance unless otherwise noted. wof = width of fabric

Refer to Hexagon Basics on pages 8-63 before beginning the project.

Cutting

Note: Use the holes in the templates to mark the 1/4" seam on the wrong side of the diamonds, triangles and half diamonds.

From light print fabrics, cut:
210 diamonds using the template on page 23.
12 triangles using the template on page 24.

From medium print fabric, cut:
204 diamonds using the template on page 23.
24 half diamonds using the template on page 23.

From backing fabric, cut:
(2) equal lengths, removing the selvages.

From binding fabric, cut:
(8) 2-1/2" x wof strips.

Method

1. Lay out two light print and 2 medium print diamonds as shown.

Tumbling Stars Quilt continued

2. Sew the diamonds, right sides together, in light/medium pairs. Press seams open.

3. Layer the diamond pairs, right sides together, matching and pinning the center seam at the top.

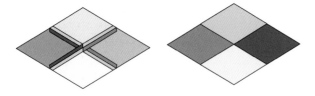

4. Sew the diamond pairs together. Press the seam open to make a large diamond unit. Make a total of 99 large diamond units.

5. Lay out three large diamond units as show.

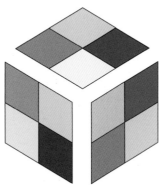

6. Layer the bottom two diamond units, right sides together, and begin sewing at the raw edge of the narrow point. Stitch toward the wider angle, stopping at the 1/4" mark on the opposite edge. Press the seam open.

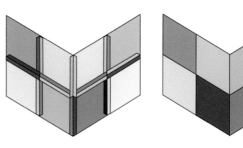

7. With right sides together, place the third diamond unit on the sewn diamonds in step 6, matching raw edges. With the third diamond unit on the bottom, sew from the raw outer fabric edge to the 1/4" mark above the open seam.

8. Leaving the needle in the work, lift the presser foot and pivot the top piece so it aligns with the raw edge of the diamond underneath. Lower the presser foot and continue to stitch to the end of the seam. Press seams open to make a hexagon. Repeat to make a total of 27 hexagons.

Note: When you pivot the diamonds, tug the top pieces backward slightly so as not to create a pleat in the seam.

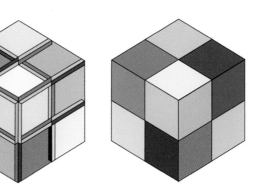

Tumbling Stars Quilt continued

9. Lay out one light print diamond and two medium print half diamonds as shown. Sew the pieces together, pressing the seams open to make a side unit. Make a total of 12 side units.

10. Lay out one medium print diamond and two light print triangles. Sew the pieces together, pressing the seams open to make a triangle section. Make a total of 6 triangle sections.

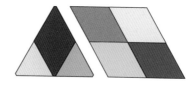

11. Lay out one large diamond unit and one triangle section as shown. Sew the pieces together, pressing the seam open to make a side unit. Make a total of 3 top half hexagons and 3 bottom half hexagons. Note the different placements on the top and bottom half hexagons.

Top half hexagon

Bottom half hexagon

Tumbling Stars Quilt continued

12. Referring to the diagram, lay out the hexagons, half hexagons and large diamond units in 6 vertical rows as shown. Rows 1, 3 and 5 have 5 hexagons and a top and bottom half hexagon. Rows 2 and 4 have 6 hexagons. Row 6 is made up of 12 large diamond units.

13. Sew the pieces, right sides together, in rows. Start and stop sewing at the 1/4" marks on the wrong side of the pieces. Press all seams open.

14. Sew the rows together pivoting at the 1/4" marks to set in each piece. Refer to Machine Sewing Hexagons on pages 38-41 for more information. As the rows are sewn together, press them in alternating directions.

Note: When sewing the rows together I find it helps to have one row draped over my shoulder as I feed them into the sewing machine. This keeps the rows from getting bunched up as they are fed under the presser foot.

15. Referring to Straightening Hexagon Quilt Edges with Inserts on pages 50-52, set in the side units on the left and right side of the quilt top.

16. Sew the 2 backing pieces, right sides together, along one long edge using a 1/2" seam allowance. Press the seam open.

17. Layer the backing, batting and quilt top together. Baste the layers together using your favorite basting technique.

18. Quilt as desired. The Tumbling Stars quilt was machine quilted in an allover loop design. Refer to pages 64-69 for more ideas on quilting hexagon quilts.

19. Trim the backing and batting even with the quilt top.

Left Side   Right Side

20. Sew the binding strips together on the diagonal to make one long continuous strip. Press the strip in half, wrong sides together, along the length.

21. Sew the binding to the quilt referring to pages 59-63.

Tumbling Stars Quilt

Finished Quilt Size: 64" x 84"

Stars and Cubes Quilt

Finished Quilt Size: 69-1/2" x 72-1/2"

Making this impressive quilt was the perfect way to use up my stash of precut 2-1/2" strips. While the quilt design seems daunting, there are no templates and only one basic shape to cut which makes it one of the easiest projects in the book.

Fabric Requirements

(36) 2-1/2" x wof multi-colored fabric strips OR
   2-1/2 yards (2.4m) assorted fabrics

Note: The more prints you use the easier it is to put the design together without too much thought on placement of specific prints. Large print fabrics provide great variation when cut up.

(9) 2-1/2" x wof assorted navy fabric strips OR
   5/8 yard (.6m) assorted navy fabrics

Note: I used a variety of navy print fabrics, but one fabric can be used for continuity.

2-1/2 yards (2.4m) white fabric

4-1/2 yards (4.1m) backing fabric

1 yard (1m) binding fabric

79" x 82" batting

- -

Fabric quantities are based on 40" usable width of fabric. Sew with a 1/4" seam allowance unless otherwise noted. wof = width of fabric

Refer to Hexagon Basics on pages 8-63 before beginning the project.

Cutting

From white fabric, cut:
   (36) 2-1/2" x wof strips

From backing fabric, cut:
   (2) equal lengths, removing the selvages.

From binding fabric, cut:
   2-1/2" bias strips to equal approximately 330".

Method

1. Lay out (2) 2-1/2" x wof multi-colored fabric strips and (1) 2-1/2" x wof white fabric strip, staggering the ends as shown.

2. Sew the strips together to make strip set A. Press seams toward print fabrics. Make 18 strip set A.

3. Align the ruler's 60-degree line on the bottom raw edge of strip set A. Cut along the right edge of the ruler to trim the ends.

Stars and Cubes Quilt continued

4. Align the 2-1/2" mark on the ruler with the left angled edge of strip set A. Cut along the right edge of the ruler to make a 2-1/2" segment. Continue cutting at 2-1/2" increments to cut a total of (252) 2-1/2" A segments from the strip sets. Each strip set should yield 14 segments.

5. Lay out (2) 2-1/2" x wof white fabric strips and (1) 2-1/2" x wof navy fabric strip, staggering the ends as shown.

6. Referring to steps 2-4, make 9 strip set B. Cut (126) 2-1/2" B segments from the strip sets.

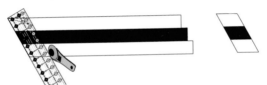

7. Lay out 2 A segments and 1 B segment as shown.

8. Stitch the segments together to make a large diamond. Press the seams open. Make a total of 118 large diamonds. Using the diamond template on page 23, mark 1/4" seams on the wrong side of the diamonds.

Note: Six of the large diamonds will be used as fillers for the sides of the quilt top.

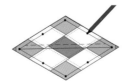

9. Lay out 6 large diamonds in a star shape as shown.

10. Layer two of the diamonds, right sides together, and begin sewing at the raw edge of the narrow point. Stitch toward the wider angle, stopping at the 1/4" mark on the opposite edge. Press the seam open. Repeat with another pair of diamonds.

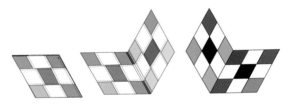

11. Layer a diamond and diamond pair, right sides together, and begin sewing at the raw edge of the narrow point. Stitch toward the wider angle, stopping at the 1/4" mark on the opposite edge to make a star half. Press the seam open. Repeat with another diamond and the remaining diamond pair.

Stars and Cubes Quilt continued

12. Sew the two star halves together. Start and stop stitching at the 1/4" marks. Press the seam open to make a star.

13. Lay out the star and 6 large diamonds as shown.

14. With right sides together, place a large diamond on the star, matching raw edges. With the diamond on the bottom, sew from the raw outer fabric edge to the 1/4" mark above the open seam.

15. Leaving the needle in the work, lift the presser foot and pivot the top piece so it aligns with the raw edge of the diamond underneath. Lower the presser foot and continue to stitch to the end of the seam. Press seams away from the star point of the next inset diamond.

Note: When you pivot the work, tug the top pieces backward slightly so as not to create a pleat in the seam.

16. Insert the remaining diamonds to make a hexagon. Press the seams in the same direction. Make a total of 7 hexagons.

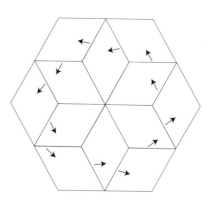

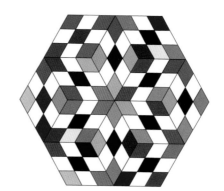

Stars and Cubes Quilt continued

17. To make the half hexagons, lay out 7 large
    diamonds as shown. Referring to steps 10-11,
    make a star half.

18. Referring to steps 14-15, inset the remaining
    diamonds into the star half. Press seams open.

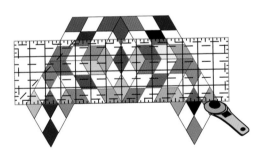

19. Trim the ends of the diamonds to make a
    straight edge. Repeat to make a total of 4
    half hexagons.

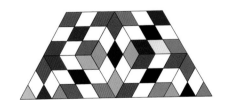

Stars and Cubes Quilt continued

20. Lay out the half hexagons and full hexagons in 3 vertical rows as shown. The outside rows each have 2 half and 2 full hexagons. The center row has 3 full hexagons.

21. Sew the hexagons, right sides together, in rows. Start and stop sewing at the 1/4" marks on the wrong side of the hexagons. Press all seams open.

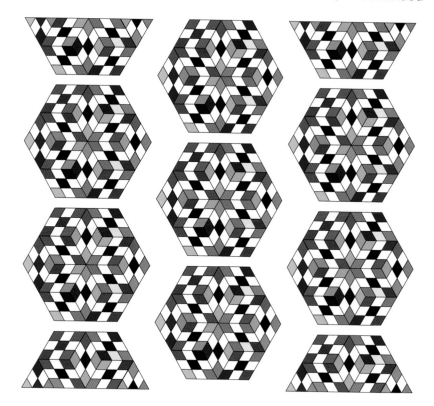

22. Sew the rows together pivoting at the 1/4" marks to set in each hexagon. Refer to Machine Sewing Hexagons on pages 38-41 for more information. Sew through the seam allowances at the top and bottom of the quilt.

23. As the rows are sewn together, press them in alternating directions.

Note: It is not necessary to press the seams open since the top and bottom of the quilt are straight edges and the side seams are already pressed open.

Stars and Cubes Quilt continued

24. To complete the quilt top, set in 3 diamonds on the left and right side of the quilt top. Refer to Machine Sewing Hexagons on pages 38-41 for more information. Press seams open.

25. Sew the 2 backing pieces, right sides together, along one long edge using a 1/2" seam allowance. Press the seam open.

26. Layer the backing, batting and quilt top together. Baste the layers together using your favorite basting technique.

27. Quilt as desired. The Stars and Cubes quilt was machine quilted in an all over vermicelli design. Refer to pages 64-69 for more ideas on quilting hexagon quilts.

28. Trim the backing and batting even with the quilt top.

29. Sew the bias binding strips together on the diagonal to make one long continuous strip. Press the strip in half, wrong sides together, along the length.

30. Sew the bias binding to the quilt referring to pages 59-63.

Stars and Cubes Quilt

Finished Quilt Size: 69-1/2" x 72-1/2"

Boxed Hexagon Quilt

Finished Quilt Size: 71" x 77"

I have long admired this 1930's patchwork design. Some leftover hexagons inspired me to stitch my own version. I knew I wanted to sew this quilt by hand since there were so many set in pieces, but I wanted to do some machine stitching to move the process along. I decided to stitch all the stars on the sewing machine and set in the filler diamonds and hexagons by hand. It was the best of both worlds for me.

Fabric Requirements

3-5/8 yards (3.3m) assorted light print fabric
   for hexagons

3-1/4 yards (3m) assorted medium print fabric
   for stars

3/4 yard (.7m) assorted medium to dark fabric for
   filler diamonds

4-7/8 yards (4.5m) backing fabric

5/8 yard (.6m) binding fabric

81" x 87" batting

- -

Fabric quantities are based on 40" usable width of fabric.
Sew with a 1/4" seam allowance unless otherwise noted.
wof = width of fabric

Refer to Hexagon Basics on pages 8-63
before beginning the project.

Cutting

Note: Use the holes in the templates to mark the
   1/4" seam on the wrong side of the hexagons.
   Use a ruler to mark the 1/4" seam on the wrong
   side of the diamonds.

From assorted light print fabric, cut:
   53 hexagons using the template on page 25.
   14 half hexagons using the template on page 25.

From assorted medium print fabric, cut:
   (52) 2-1/4" x wof strips. From the strips, cut:
      720 diamonds referring to Cutting
      60-degree Diamonds from 2-1/4" Strips
      on page 32.

From assorted medium to dark fabric, cut:
   (12) 2-1/4" x wof strips. From the strips, cut:
      164 filler diamonds referring to Cutting
      60-degree Diamonds from 2-1/4" Strips
      on page 32.

From backing fabric, cut:
   (2) equal lengths, removing the selvages.

From binding fabric, cut:
   (9) 2-1/2" x wof strips.

Boxed Hexagon Quilt continued

Method

1. Lay out 6 medium print diamonds in a star shape as shown. Choose 2 sets of 3 diamonds in the same fabric. Alternate the fabrics within the star.

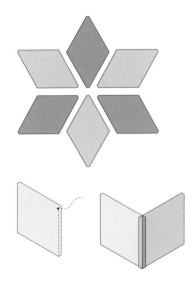

2. Layer two diamonds, right sides together, and begin sewing at the raw edge of the narrow point. Stitch toward the wider angle, stopping at the 1/4" mark on the opposite edge. Press the seam open. Repeat with another pair of diamonds stitching with the alternate fabric on top.

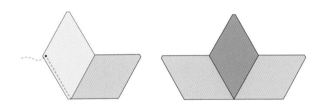

3. Layer a diamond and diamond pair, right sides together, alternating the print. Begin sewing at the raw edge of the narrow point. Stitch toward the wider angle, stopping at the 1/4" mark on the opposite edge to make a star half. Press the seam open. Repeat with the remaining diamond and diamond pair.

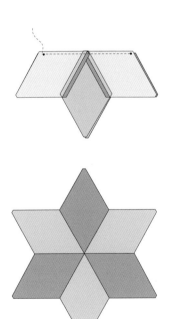

4. Sew the two star halves together. Start and stop stitching at the 1/4" marks. Press the seam open to make a star. Make a total of 120 stars.

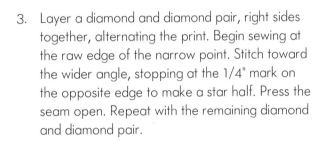

Boxed Hexagon Quilt continued

5. Lay out 15 stars and 21 filler diamonds in a row as shown.

6. Stitch the stars and filler diamonds, right sides together, in rows. Start and stop sewing at the 1/4" marks. Press the seams toward the filler diamonds to make row A. Make 4 row A.

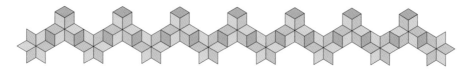

7. Lay out 15 stars and 22 filler diamonds as shown. Referring to step 6, stitch the pieces together to make row B. Make 4 row B.

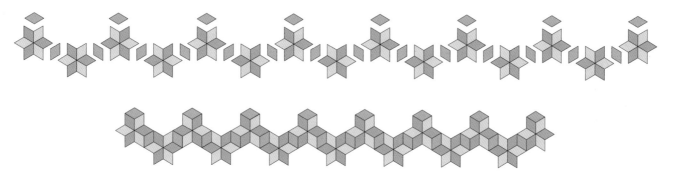

8. Lay out one row A, 7 half hexagons and 8 filler diamonds as shown.

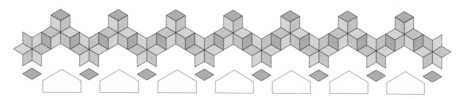

9. With right sides together, place a filler diamond on row A, matching raw edges. With the diamond on the bottom, sew from the raw outer fabric edge to the 1/4" mark above the open seam.

Boxed Hexagon Quilt continued

10. Leaving the needle in the work, lift the presser foot and pivot the top piece so it aligns with the raw edge of the diamond underneath. Lower the presser foot and continue to stitch to the end of the seam. Press seams toward the diamond.

    Note: When you pivot the work, tug the top piece backward slightly so as not to create a pleat in the seam.

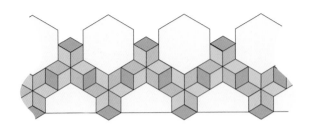

11. Continue setting in the filler diamonds and half hexagons along the bottom of row A. Set in full hexagons to the top of row A. This is the bottom row of the quilt top.

12. Work your way up the quilt top, adding row B, hexagons, row A, hexagons and so on. Work in this way building up the quilt finishing with row B at the top edge. Add the half hexagons and filler diamonds to this row.

Row B

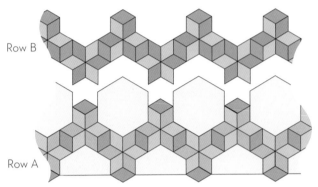

Row A

13. Trim along the edges where the hexagons and diamonds extend beyond the quilt top.

14. Sew the 2 backing pieces, right sides together, along one long edge using a 1/2" seam allowance. Press the seam open.

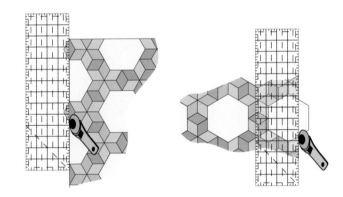

15. Layer the backing, batting and quilt top together. Baste the layers together using your favorite basting technique.

16. Quilt as desired. The Boxed Hexagon quilt was machine quilted in an all over vermicelli design. Refer to pages 64-69 for more ideas on quilting hexagon quilts.

17. Trim the backing and batting even with the quilt top.

18. Sew the binding strips together on the diagonal to make one long continuous strip. Press the strip in half, wrong sides together, along the length.

19. Sew the binding to the quilt referring to pages 59-63.

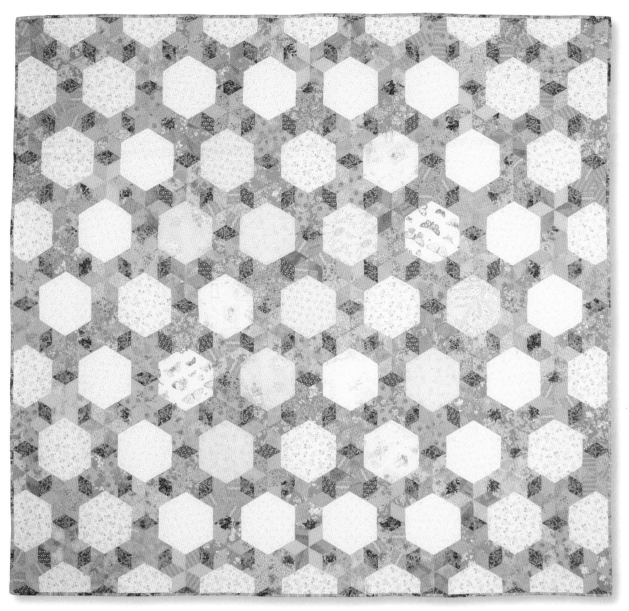

Boxed Hexagon Quilt

Finished Quilt Size: 71" x 77"

Resources

Batting
www.hobbsbatting.com

Quilting Thread
www.superiorthreads.com
www.valdani.com

Hera Marker
www.clover-usa.com

**505® Spray Baste,
404® Spray and Fix**
www.odifusa.com

Needles
www.jjneedles.com

Design Mat, Matilda's own
www.Victoriantextiles.com

Templates
www.carolynforster.co.uk

www.sew-craft.com

www.landauerpub.com

or ask for them at your local quilt shop

Books/Bibliography

Utility Quilting,
Carolyn Forster, Landauer Publishing, 2011

The Quilter Album of Patchwork Patterns,
Jinny Beyer, Breckling Press, 2009

Quiltmaking by Hand,
Jinny Beyer, Breckling Press, 2003

Quilting with Style,
Gwen Marston and Joe Cunningham,
AQS, 1993

The Scrap Look,
Jinny Beyer, EPM Publications, 1985

Star Quilts, Outside the Box,
Edie McGinnis,
Kansas City Star Books, 2001

Mosaic Quilts,
The Charleston Museum,
Curious Works Press, 2002

Elegant Geometry,
American and British Mosaic Patchwork,
International Quilt Study Centre
and Museum, 2011

Antique Ohio Amish Quilts,
The Darwin D. Bearley Collection,
Published 2006, by Bernina

Acknowledgements

As always I appreciate the amazing team Jeramy has at Landauer Publishing. Thanks for making it all so much fun.

Thanks to Craig and Paul who realize it is not all fun all the time, especially when they need feeding and laundry, and I need to sew and write.

Thanks to Chris, Ileana and Jo for the great machine quilting.

Thank you to Jennifer and Colin for working with me on the templates.

And a big thank you to my students who continue to inspire me with their questions and work.

Dedication

Margaret Myers (but still Miss Prince to me), in whose needlework class I stitched my first hexagons.

"When you know better, you do better." Maya Angelou, 1928-2014

144